DRAWN FROM HISTORY

A Cartoon Journey Through Britain's Past

JAMES MELLOR

Published by
Filament Publishing Ltd
16 Croydon Road, Beddington, Croydon,
Surrey, CR0 4PA, United Kingdom.
www.filamentpublishing.com
Telephone: +44 (0)208 688 2598

Drawn from History by James Mellor
© 2016 James Mellor
ISBN 978-1-911425-16-8

Printed by IngramSpark

Foreword

© Jamie Huges
www.jamiehughesphotography.com

I love this book; bringing history to life through cartoons is genius.

Gregg Wallace
From BBC's MasterChef

Testimonials

"Often everyday situations are cast in a whole new light with James' dry wit and ability to see things from a different perspective. With the use of subtle humour, his original style and creativity make his drawings come to life and always put a smile on my face."

Lisa Thompson, Blue Acorns

"James Mellor's illustrations are sharp, funny, and with an original slant. He has economy of line and an abundance of humour. Excellent!"

Paul Leacy, Insight Security

"James' cartoons are simple and witty with key messages that really make you think ... and laugh."

Lisa de Garston, Prism Brain Mapping

Acknowledgements

I could thank the eclectic cast of wonderful characters from Britain's past for providing the subject matter for this book, but that would be rather pretentious. Instead I would like to thank the friends, family and JMC clients who have supported my work through the years and provided me with the confidence to create a book of my own. I would particularly like to thank my father for the valuable advice and guidance drawn from his own experience as an author.

My greatest thanks go to my amazing wife, Rachel, not just for the round-the-clock support service she operated whilst I was writing this book, but for her perpetual kindness, patience and encouragement. If I had a fraction of the belief in me that she does, I would fly.

Hera the cat has provided no help whatsoever, yet somehow she's the one who's ended up with a cameo in Chapter 9.

James Mellor is a freelance writer and cartoonist. He launched his company James Mellor Creative in 2012 to help people turn their ideas into usable, engaging and memorable content. The business is built around his three areas of expertise, research, writing and cartoon illustration, deployed either independently or in combination. In these areas, he has worked with large institutions, SMEs, start-ups and individuals to get their unique messages across in print, online and via social media.

Those who follow @jamesdfmellor on Twitter will be aware that historical figures and events often creep into his cartoon commentaries of the day's events and his illustrations are popular with teachers as resources for history lessons. There are rumours that his pictures are popular with their students too.

A history graduate from the University of York, James has always possessed a passion for the past. *Drawn From History* is James' first book and has allowed him to fully deploy his professional cartooning ability in his favourite setting, viewing Britain's past with a sharp, sideways slant. James lives in Rushden, Northamptonshire with his wife Rachel and a small, sociopathic cat.

w: jamesmellorcreative.com   t: @jamesdfmellor   f: facebook.com/jamesmellorcreative

Table of Contents

Ancient Britain

This journey begins before Britain existed. It begins before even the component nations of Britain existed. It begins before the concept of the nation state itself. Despite this, it is still a distinctly British history.

After the land bridge to the continent melted at the end of the last Ice Age, these islands were cut off and began to carve an identity all of their own.

Much of this carving was literal carving. From artistic scratches on cave walls to the carved trilithons of Stonehenge, our ancestors clearly enjoyed making their mark in stone.

Many people have wondered about the purpose of the art and monuments which form such a distinct part of our landscape. Many theories have been proposed – some more plausible than others. However, it doesn't really matter if we don't know what these things mean. What matters is that they meant something special to the people who made them.

It can't have all been lugging great stones around though. Perhaps these same people demonstrated their latent Britishness by gathering together at four o'clock each day. Tea wouldn't be imported for another 4,700 years and the sandwich wasn't invented until 1762, but they may have sat in anticipation. Perhaps not.

Discovering that flint could make fire
quickly led to the discovery of the razor

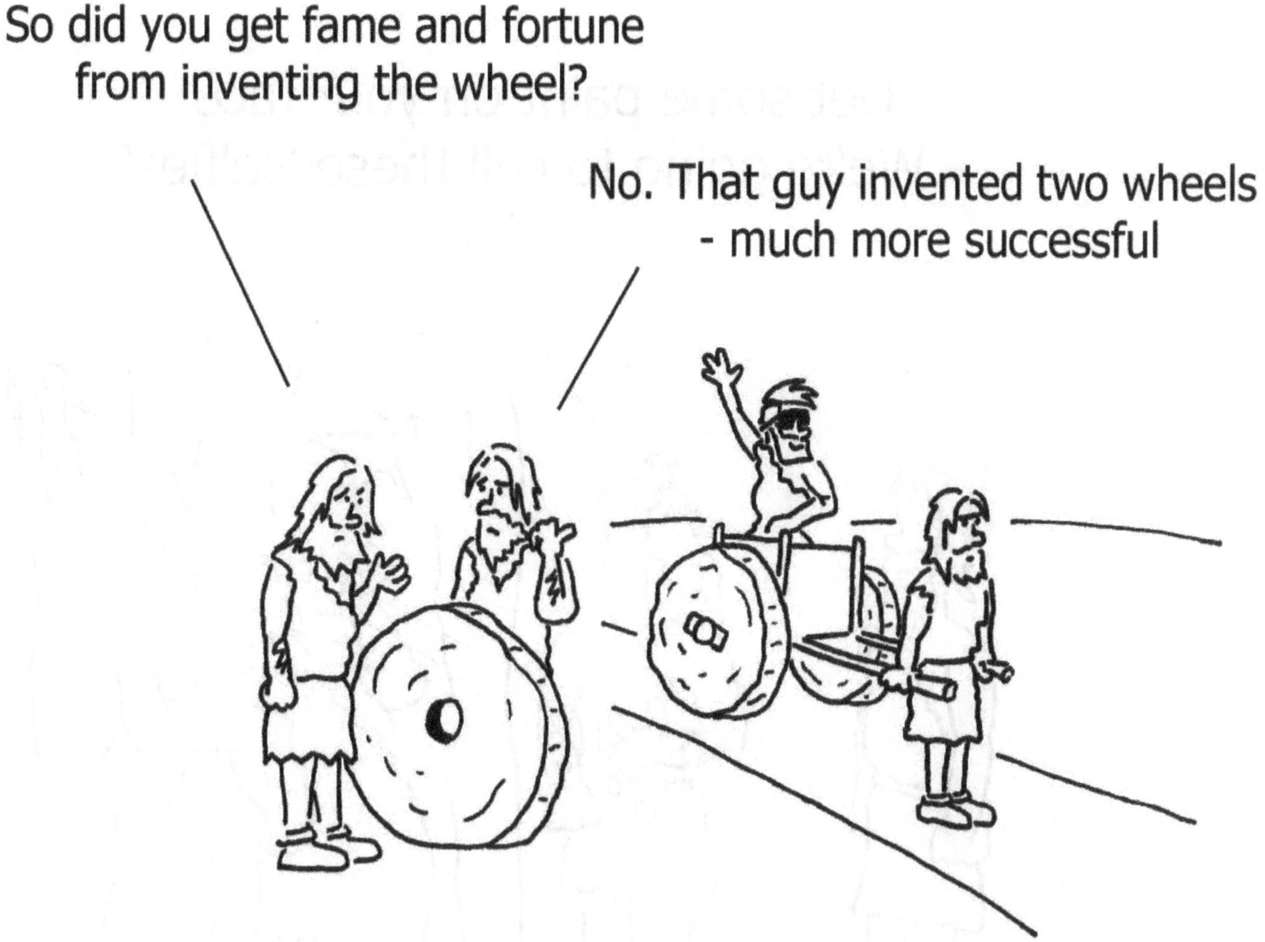
So did you get fame and fortune from inventing the wheel?
No. That guy invented two wheels - much more successful

Get some paint on your face
- We're going to call these 'selfies'

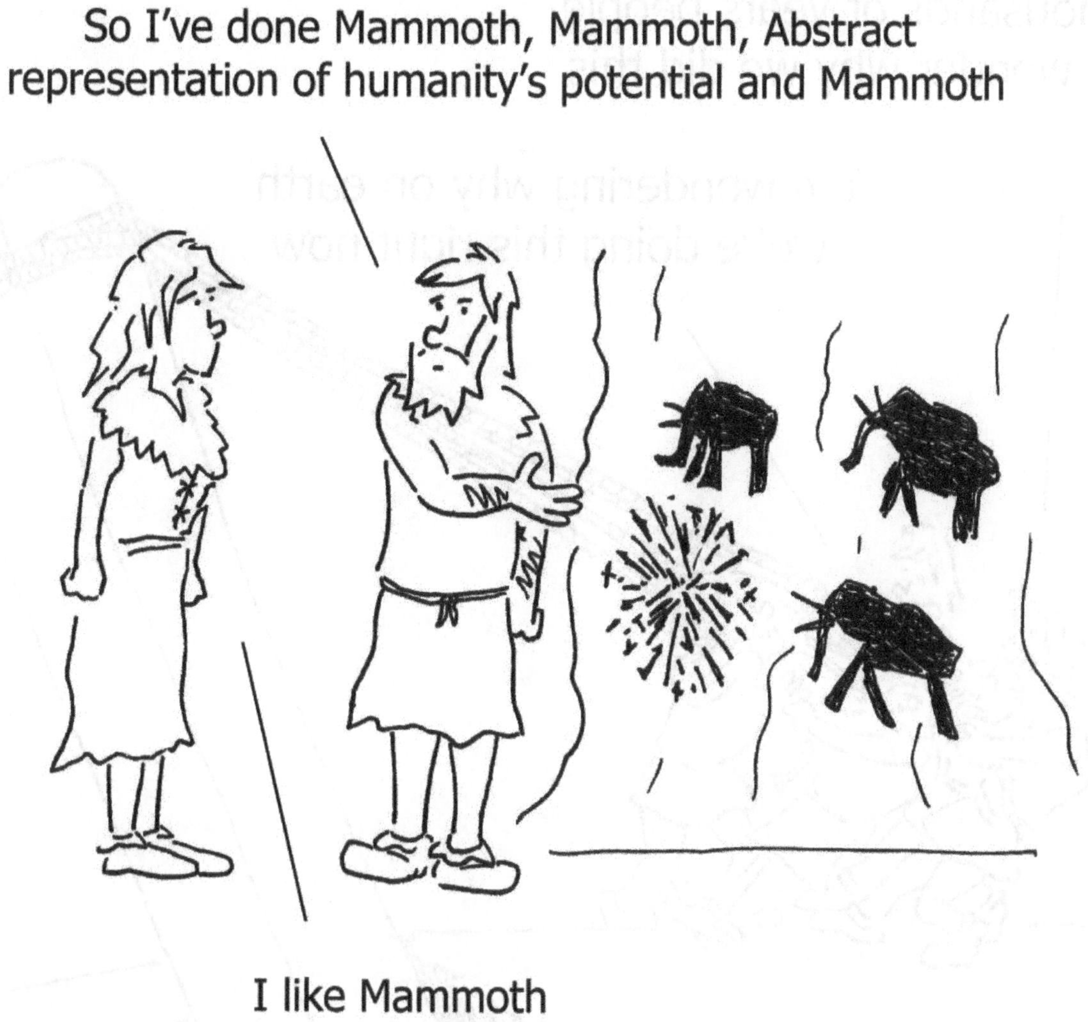
So I've done Mammoth, Mammoth, Abstract representation of humanity's potential and Mammoth
I like Mammoth

Cave Art

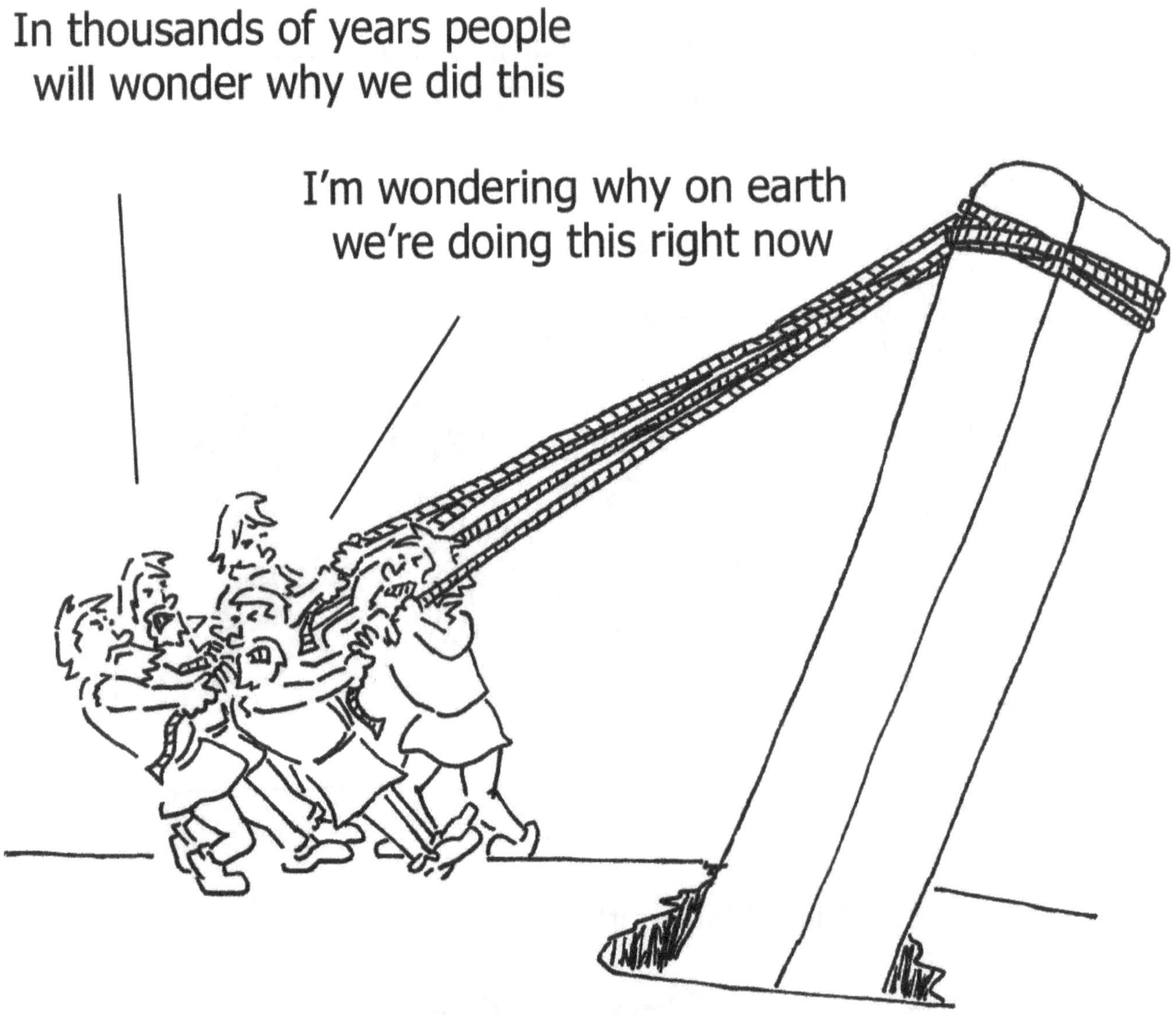
In thousands of years people will wonder why we did this
I'm wondering why on earth we're doing this right now

Building Stonehenge

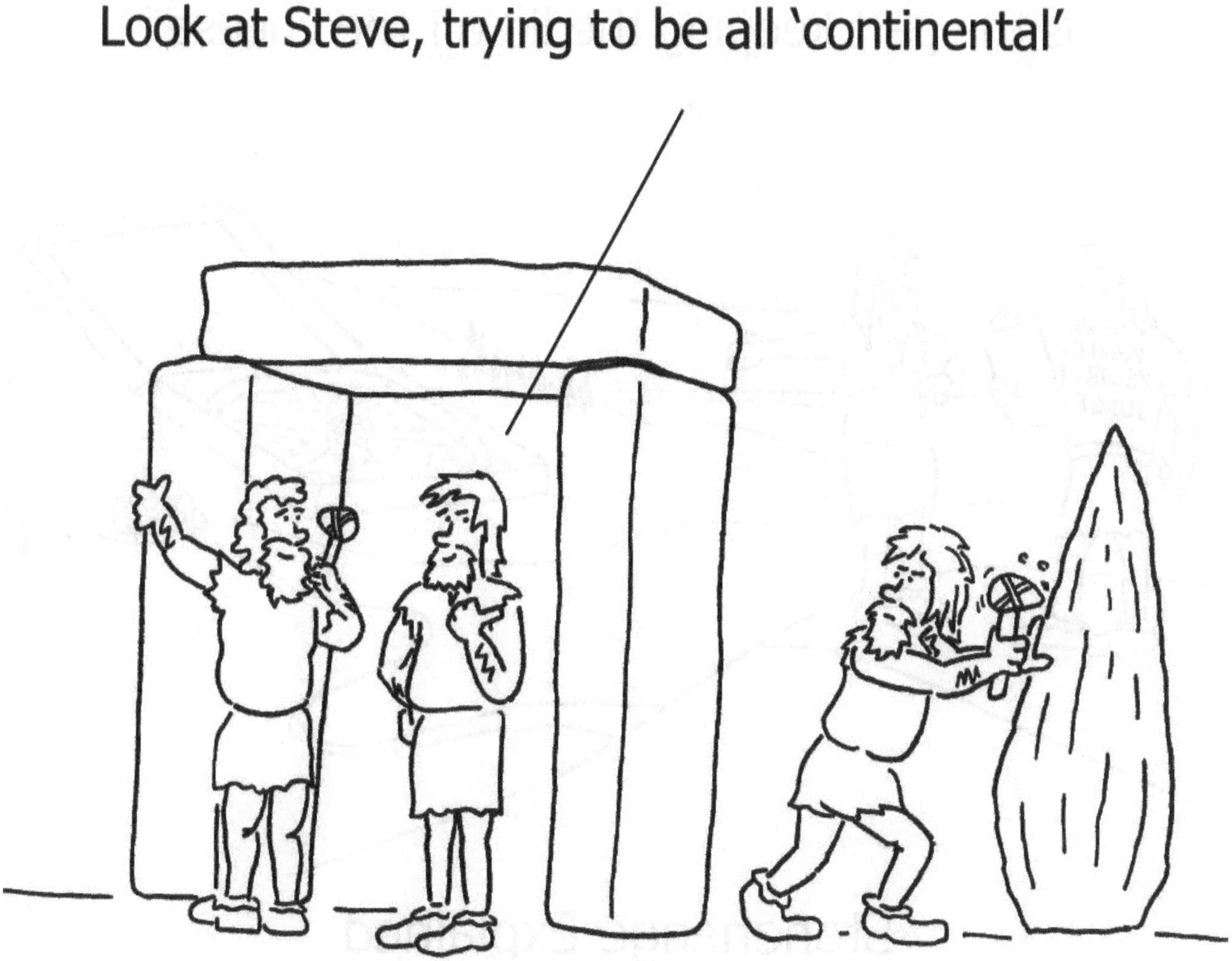
Look at Steve, trying to be all 'continental'

The really innovative aspect of
'The World's Largest Takeaway Pizza'
is the part keeping the lid off the cheese

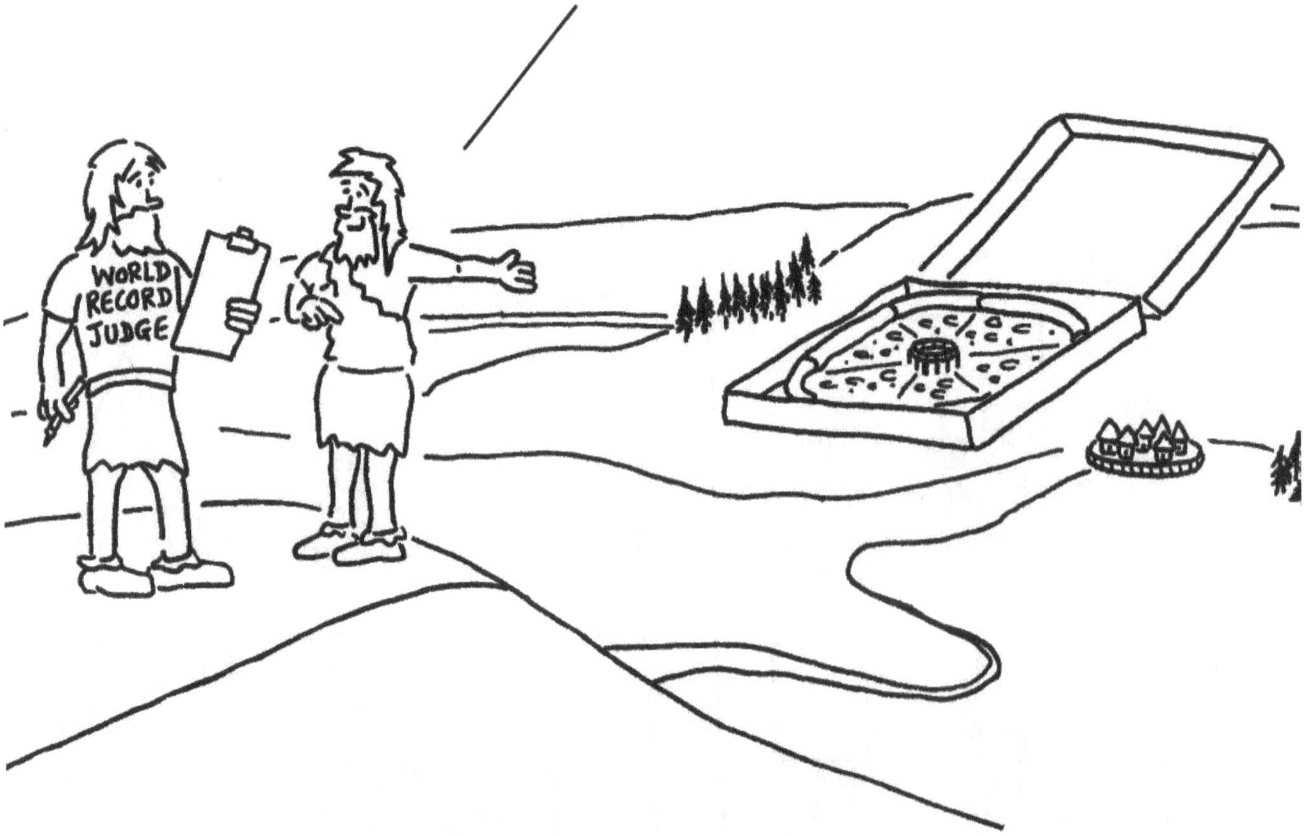
WORLD
RECORD
JUDGE

Stonehenge Explained

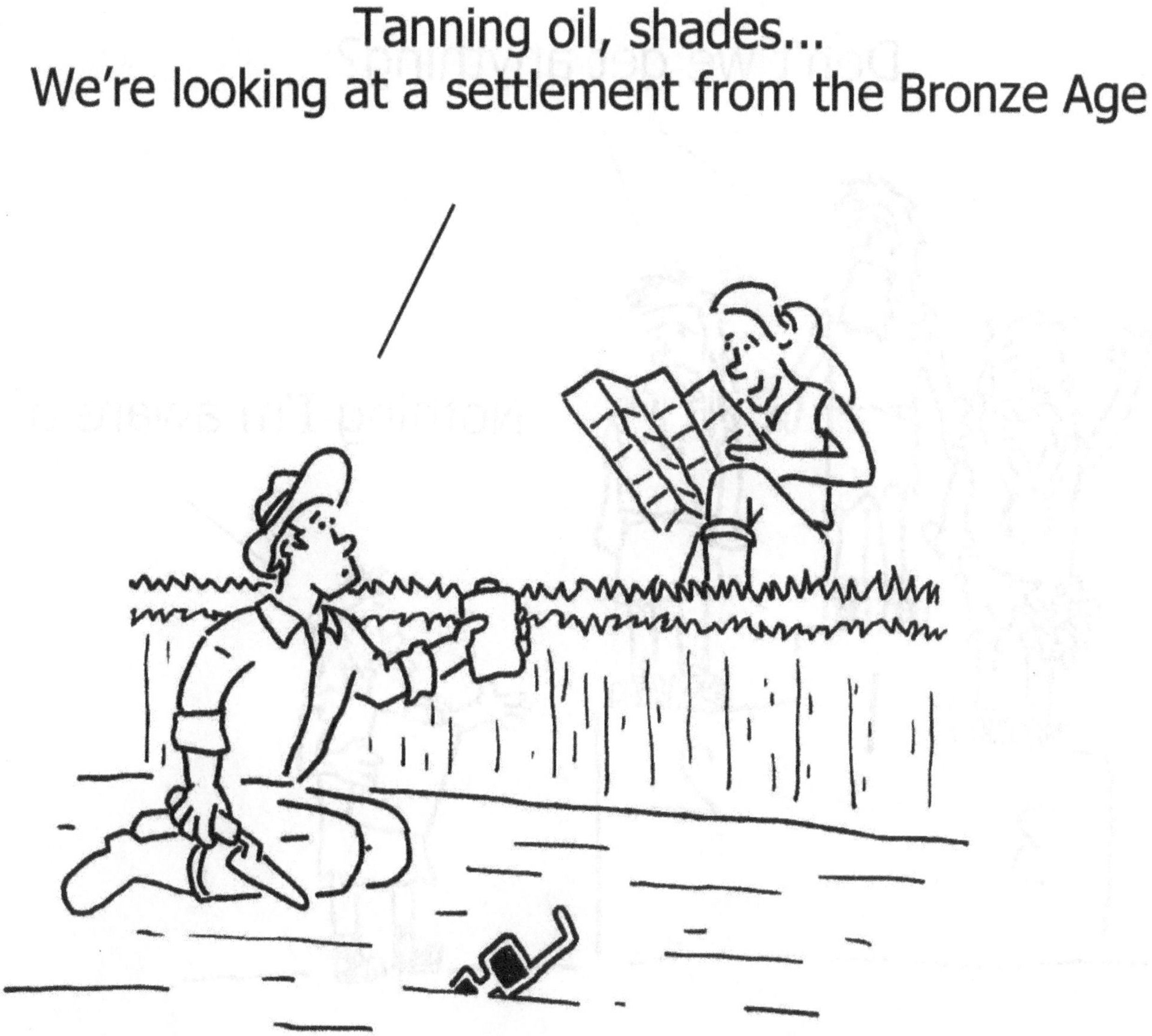
Tanning oil, shades...
We’re looking at a settlement from the Bronze Age

Archaeological Dig

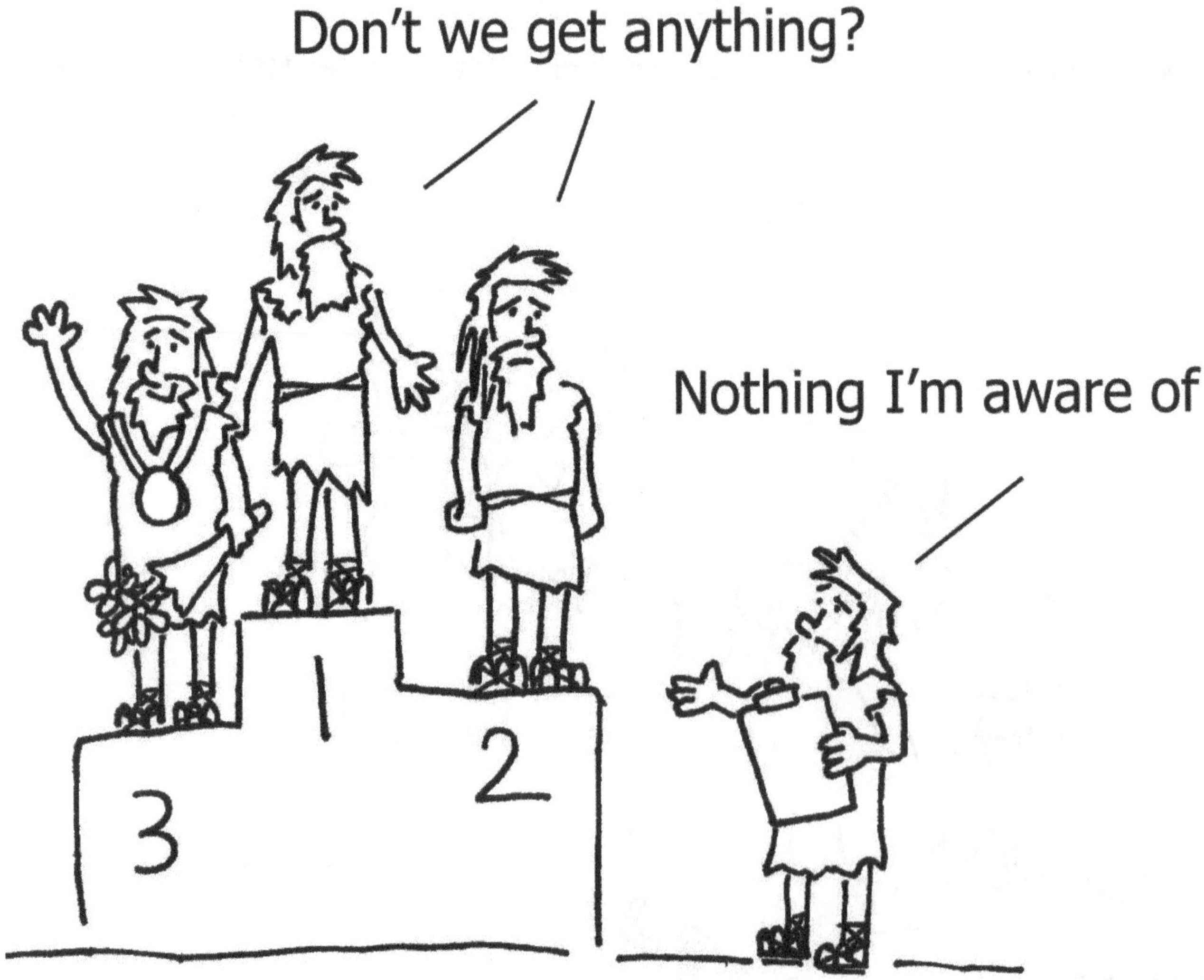
Don’t we get anything?
1
2
3
Nothing I’m aware of

Bronze Age Games

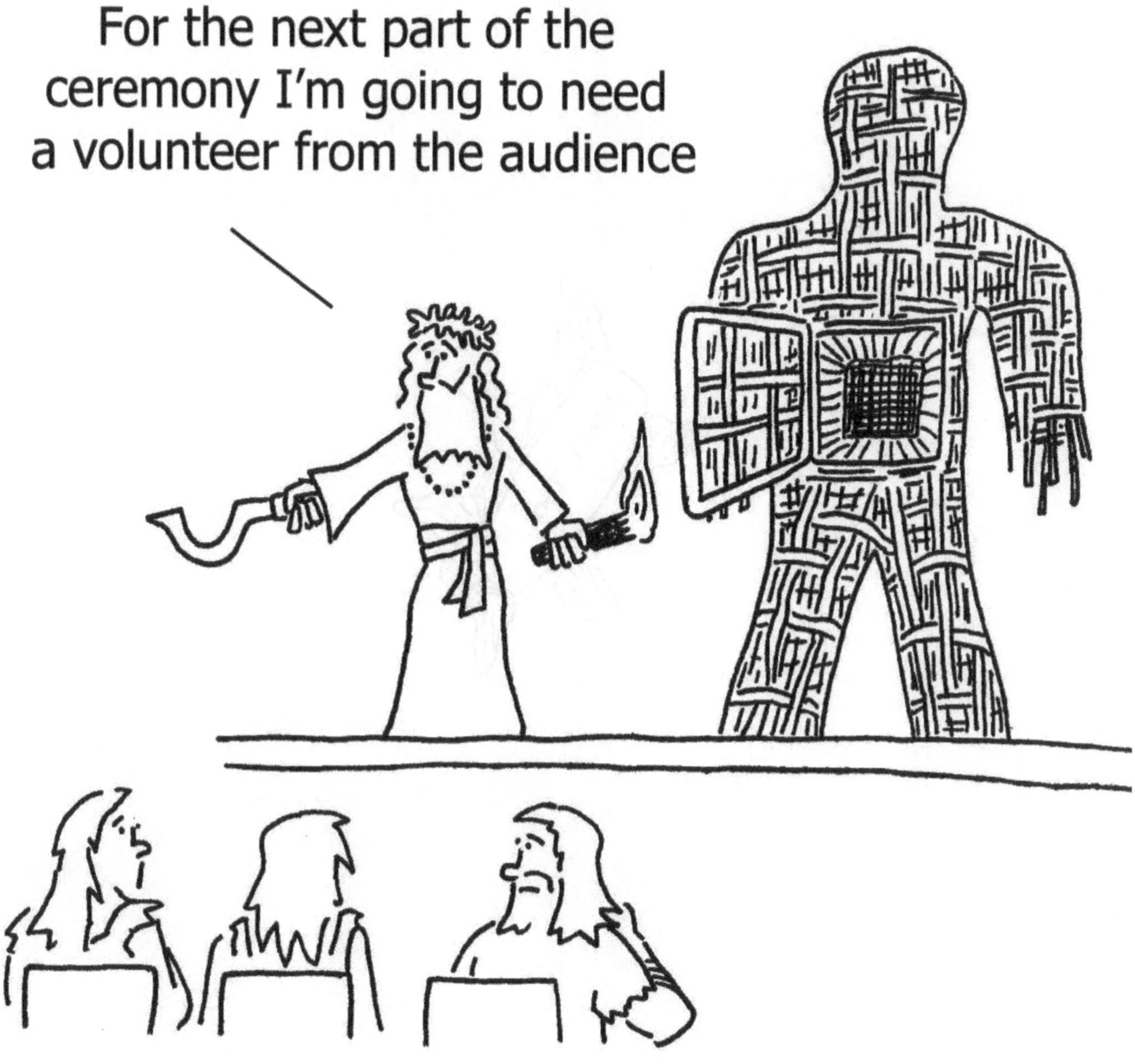
For the next part of the ceremony I'm going to need a volunteer from the audience

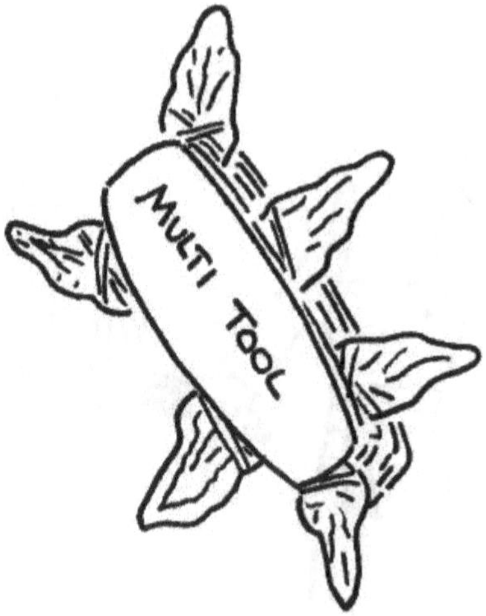
MULTI TOOL

Roman Britain

The Roman Empire extended to include Britain in AD43 and departed in AD410. Amazingly, it took the Romans over 400 years to realise that the climate in Italy was somewhat nicer than the one they found here.

Once the penny dropped that Britain was really rather drizzly and cold, they quickly packed their bags. However, their time here had an indelible impact on the culture, infrastructure and architecture of the island.

It wasn't always a happy time. Caratacus and his Catuvellauni resisted the invasion, the Iceni famously sacked Londinium and the Picts in the North got on so badly with the Romans that the invaders simply chose to wall them off.

But positive cultural exchange did take place too. The Roman Empire subsisted on Garum – a sauce made from fermented fish guts. The Empire is gone from the world, but the fish guts live on. Welsh rarebits and British Bloody Marys continue to be made with, what we now call, Worcester Sauce.

You've arrived and cut the wood.
All that's left now, Caesar, is to
play this horse chestnut game.

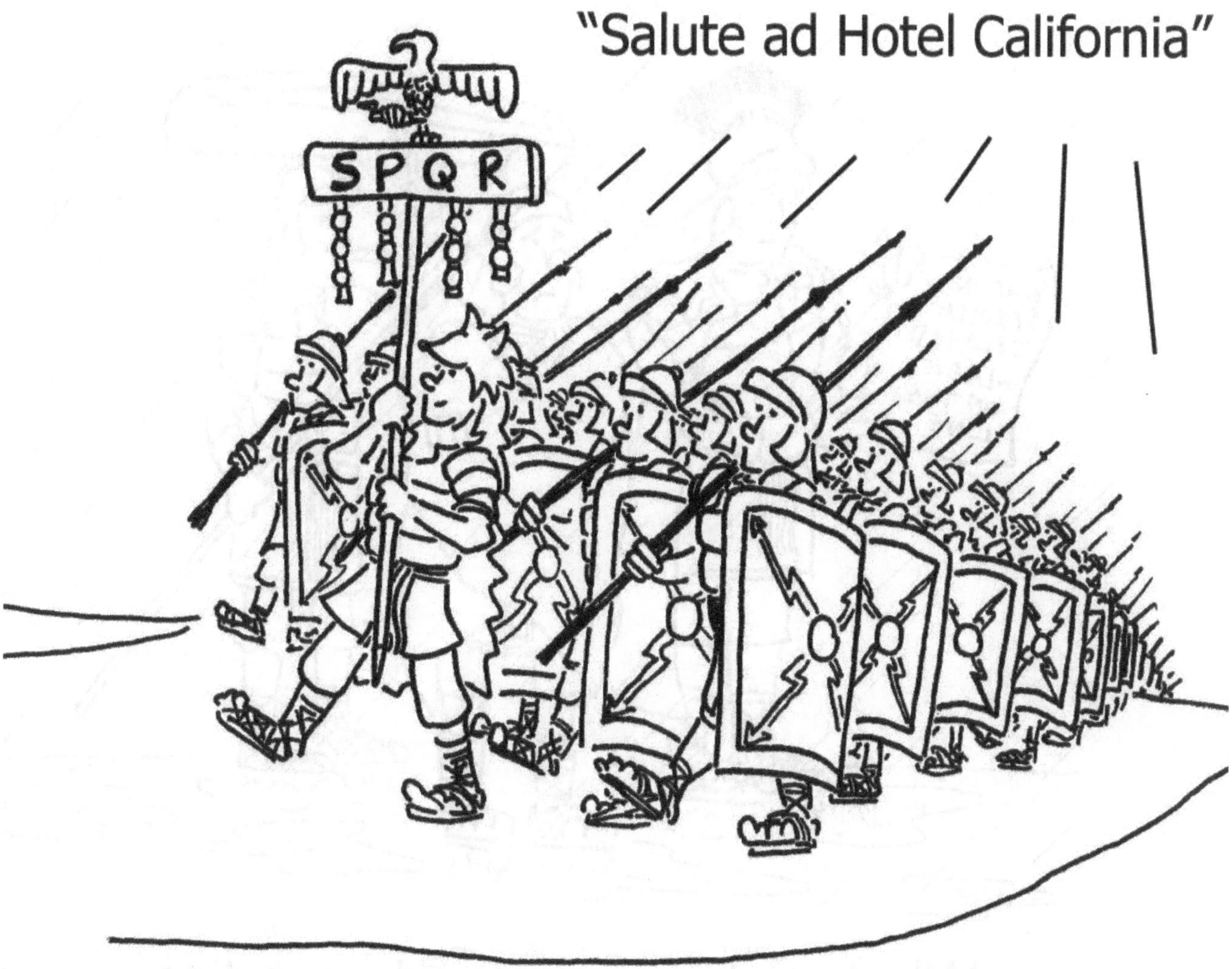
"Salute ad Hotel California"
SPQR

Britain trembled before the March of the Roman Eagles

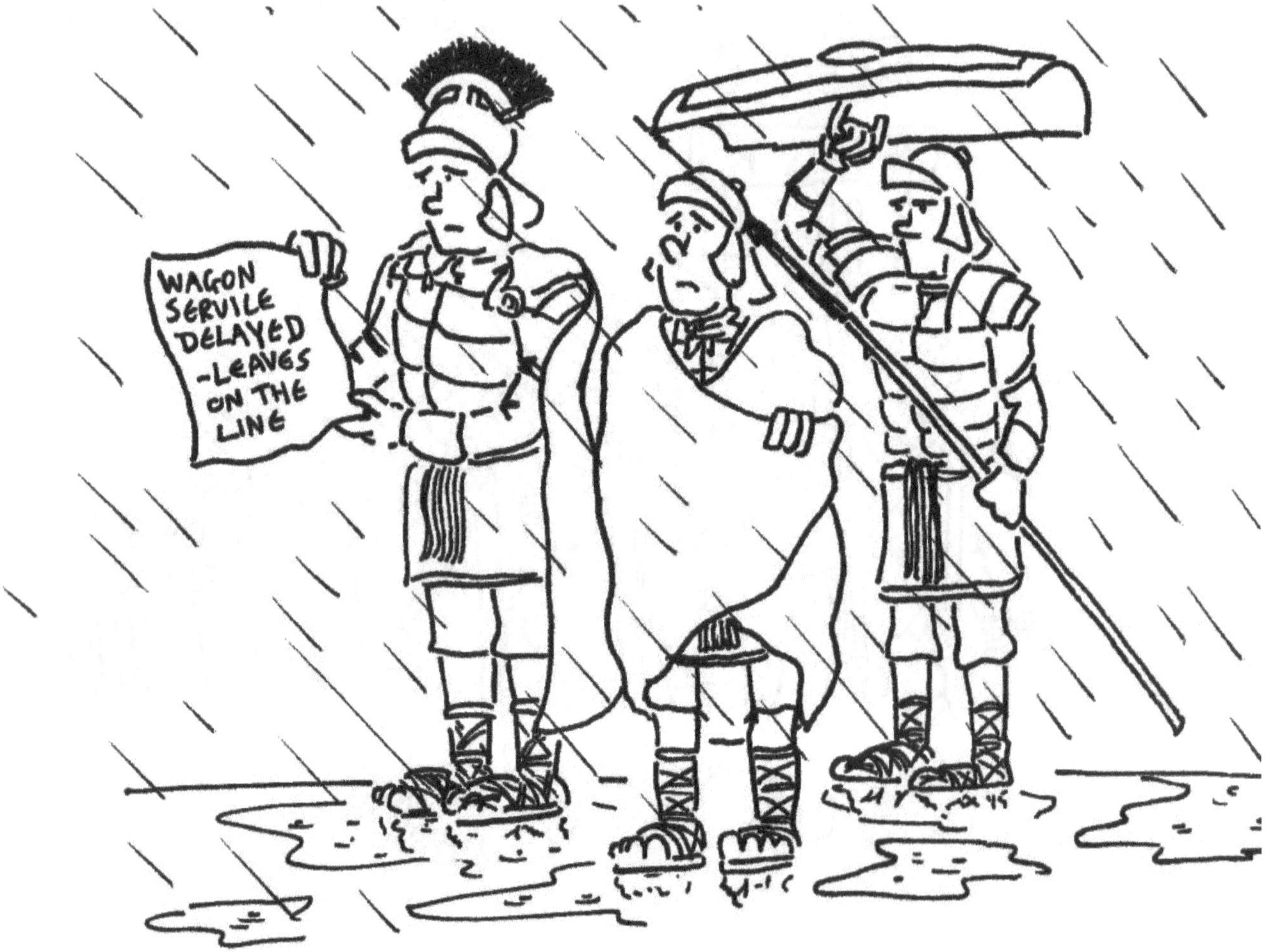
WAGON SERVICE DELAYED -LEAVES ON THE LINE

What a glorious island paradise we've added to the Empire

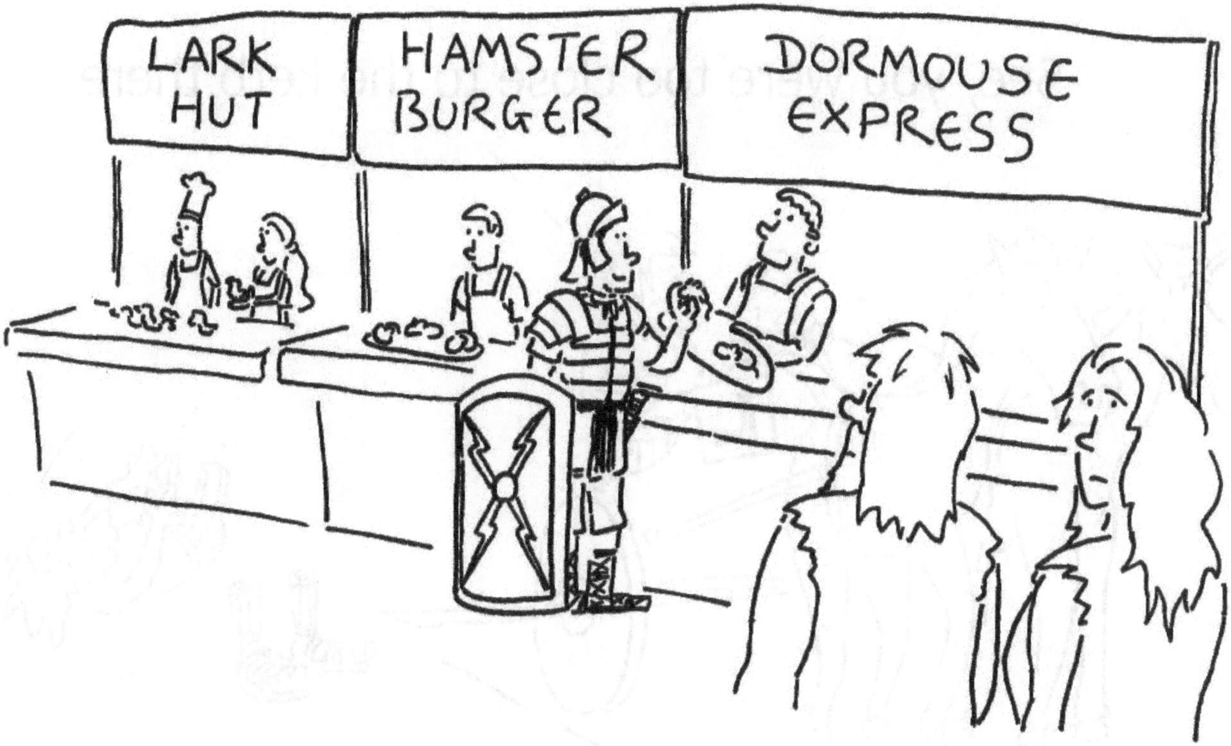
LARK HUT
HAMSTER BURGER
DORMOUSE EXPRESS

Remember before the Romans came - when this street was all pet shops not chain restaurants?

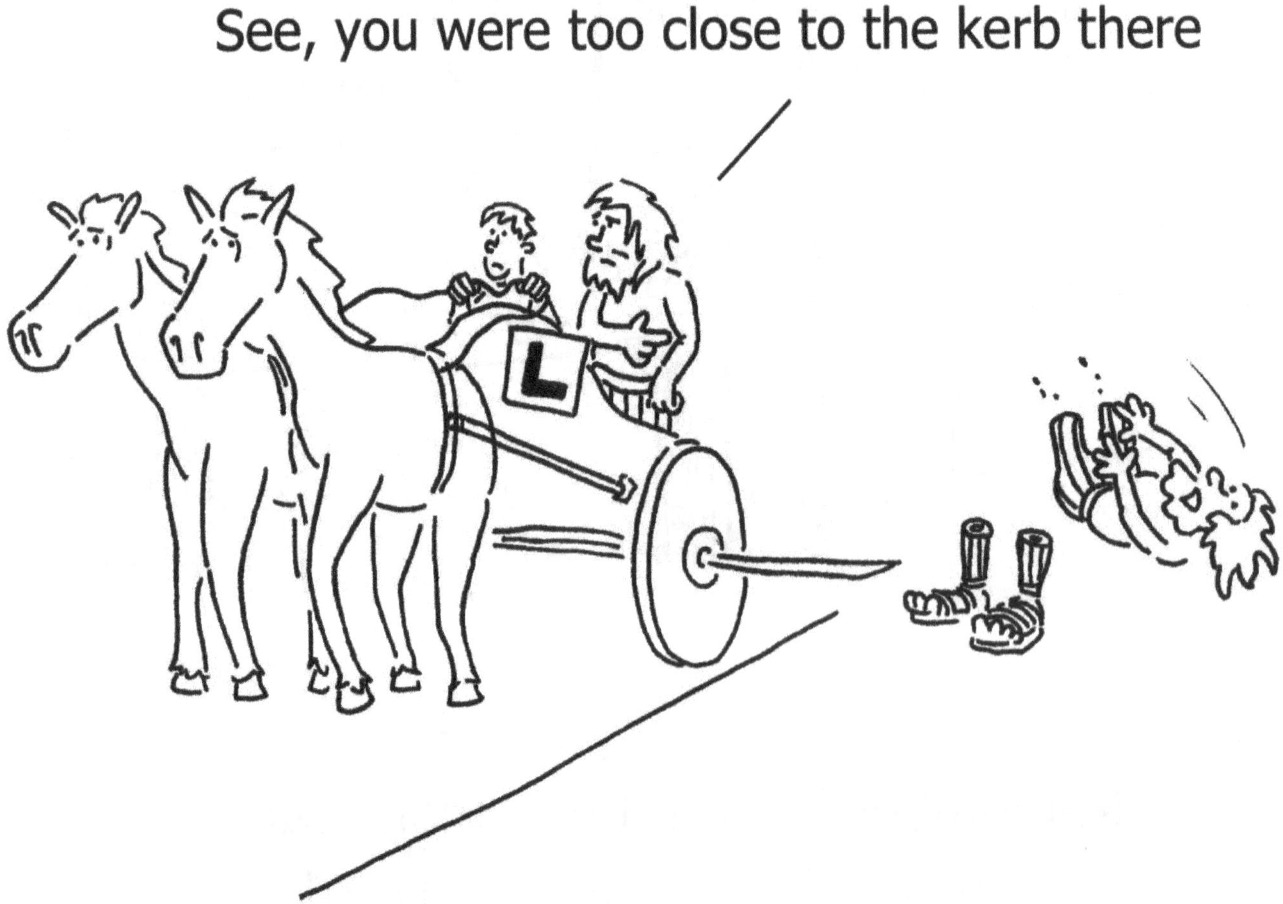
See, you were too close to the kerb there
L

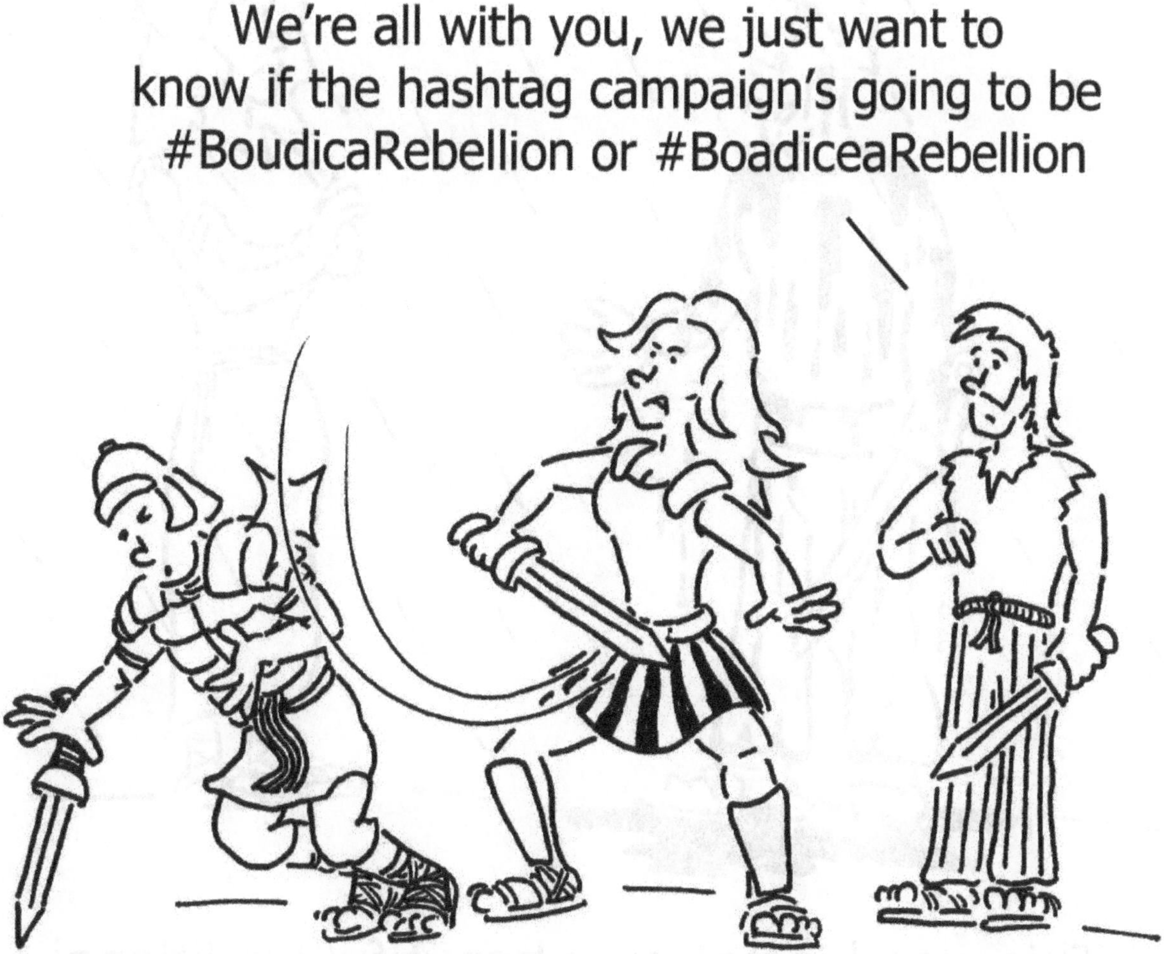
We're all with you, we just want to know if the hashtag campaign's going to be #BoudicaRebellion or #BoadiceaRebellion

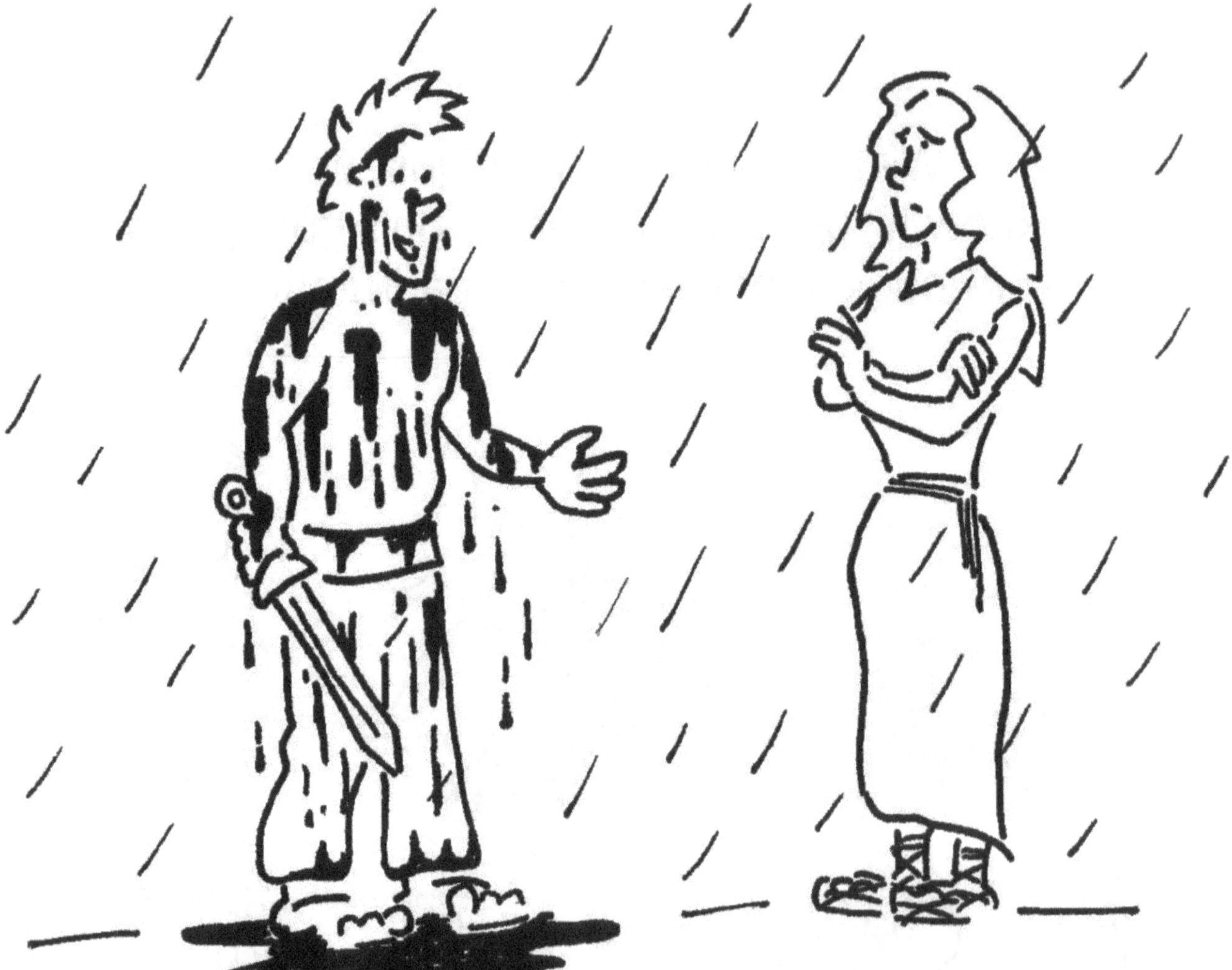

This woad is not only beautiful traditional art - it's also a powerful battle omen. When it's not raining.

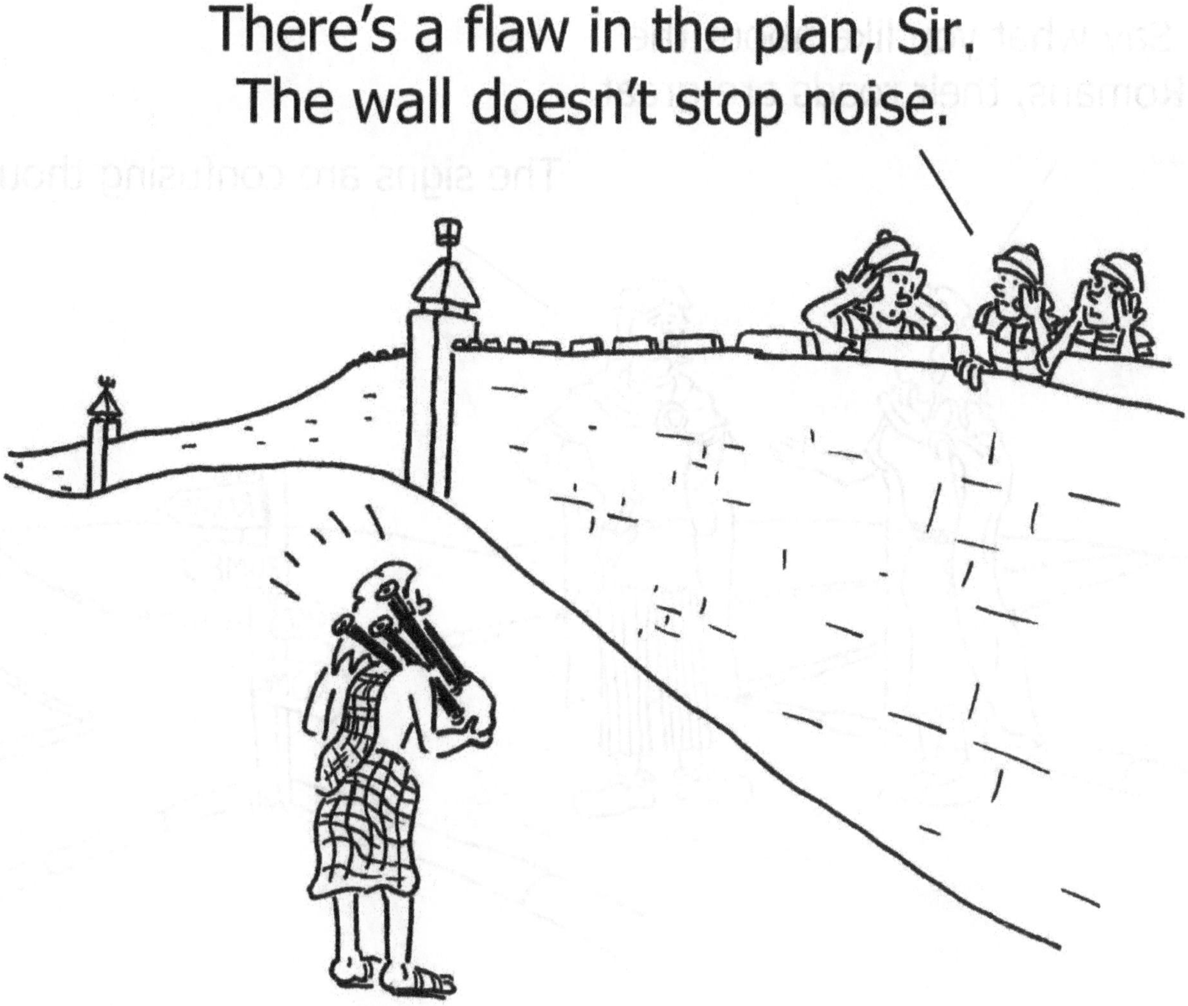
There's a flaw in the plan, Sir.
The wall doesn't stop noise.

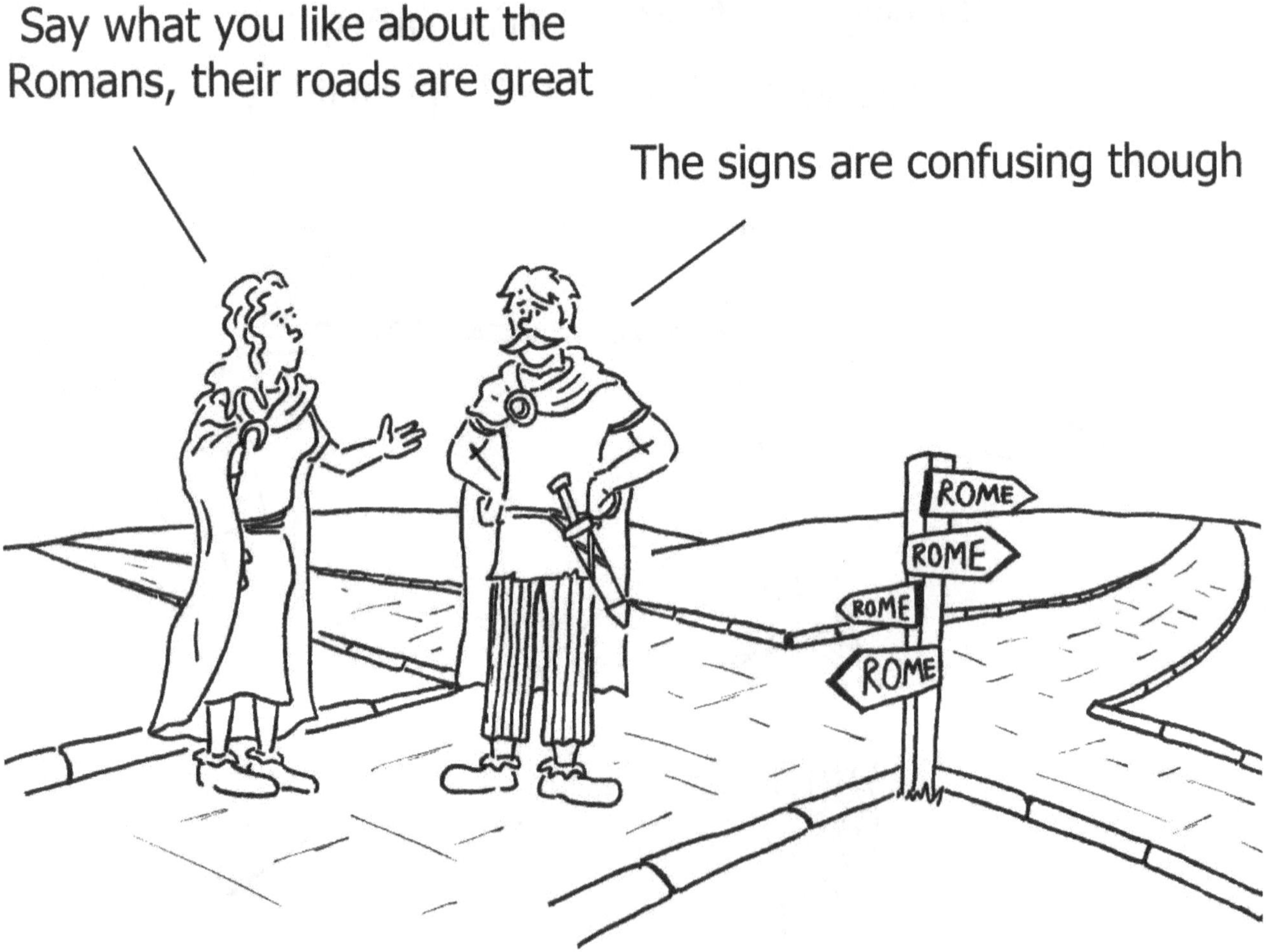
Say what you like about the Romans, their roads are great
The signs are confusing though
ROME
ROME
ROME
ROME

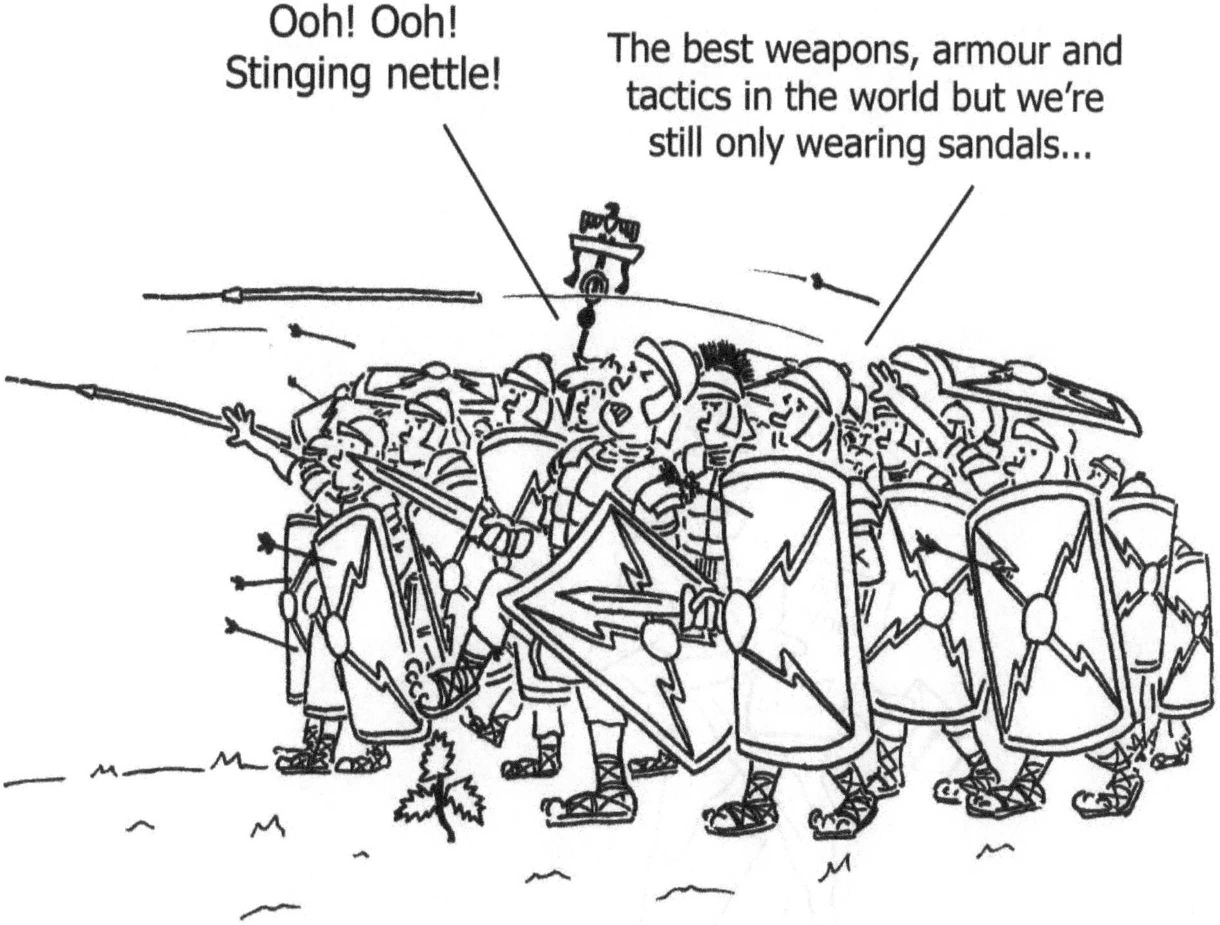
Ooh! Ooh! Stinging nettle!
The best weapons, armour and tactics in the world but we're still only wearing sandals...

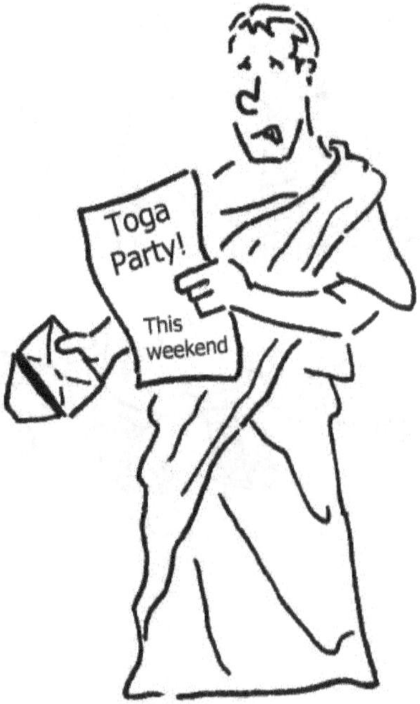
Toga
Party!
This
weekend

The Dark Ages

It isn't very popular to refer to the period between the Roman occupation of Britain and the Norman Conquest as 'The Dark Ages' anymore.

As the British Empire emerged and grew in the seventeenth and eighteenth centuries, historians began to think of empires as positive things. They therefore assumed that Britain between 410 and 1066, having been abandoned by the civilised Roman Empire, must have been a very dark place.

Now that empires are less popular, people question whether exiting one is necessarily bad. They point to the advances in art, literature and law that these so-called 'Dark Ages' brought. So this chapter is all happiness and light? Not exactly. Britain was a battleground. Jutes, Angles and Saxons raided, settled and ruled. Some were invaders, some were invited (they really were). They fought the locals and each other until a new threat appeared – the Vikings*.

Nothing unites a country like a common enemy and, versus the Norse encroachment, we begin to see a Britain we recognise.

*Everyone knows that Vikings didn't really have horns on their helmets. Everyone also knows that cartoon Vikings always do. This is a cartoon book.

Breaking Bede

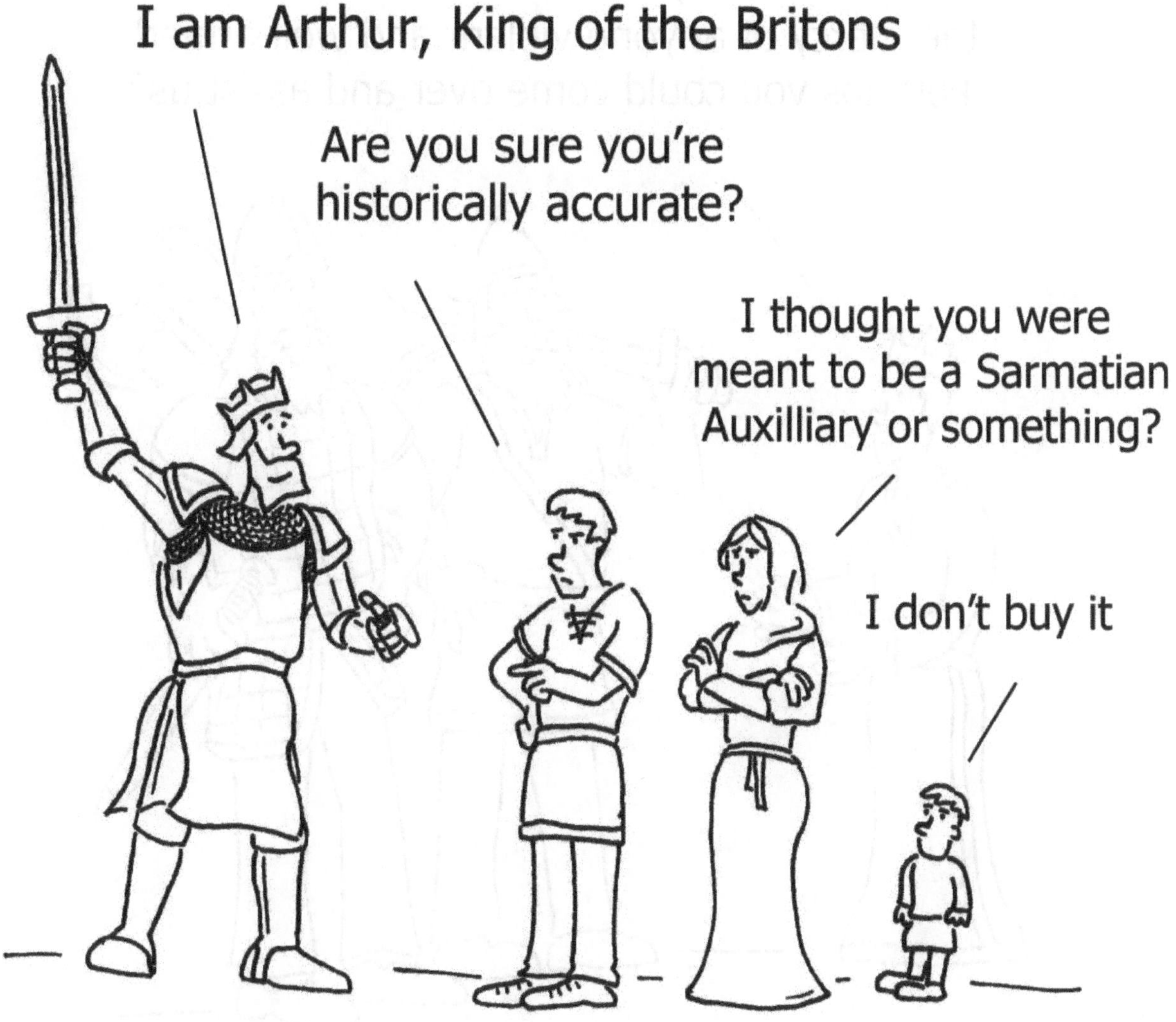
I am Arthur, King of the Britons
Are you sure you're historically accurate?
I thought you were meant to be a Sarmatian Auxilliary or something?
I don't buy it

We're a wealthy but defenceless nation - at
the mercy of anyone violent and well-armed.
Perhaps you could come over and assist us?

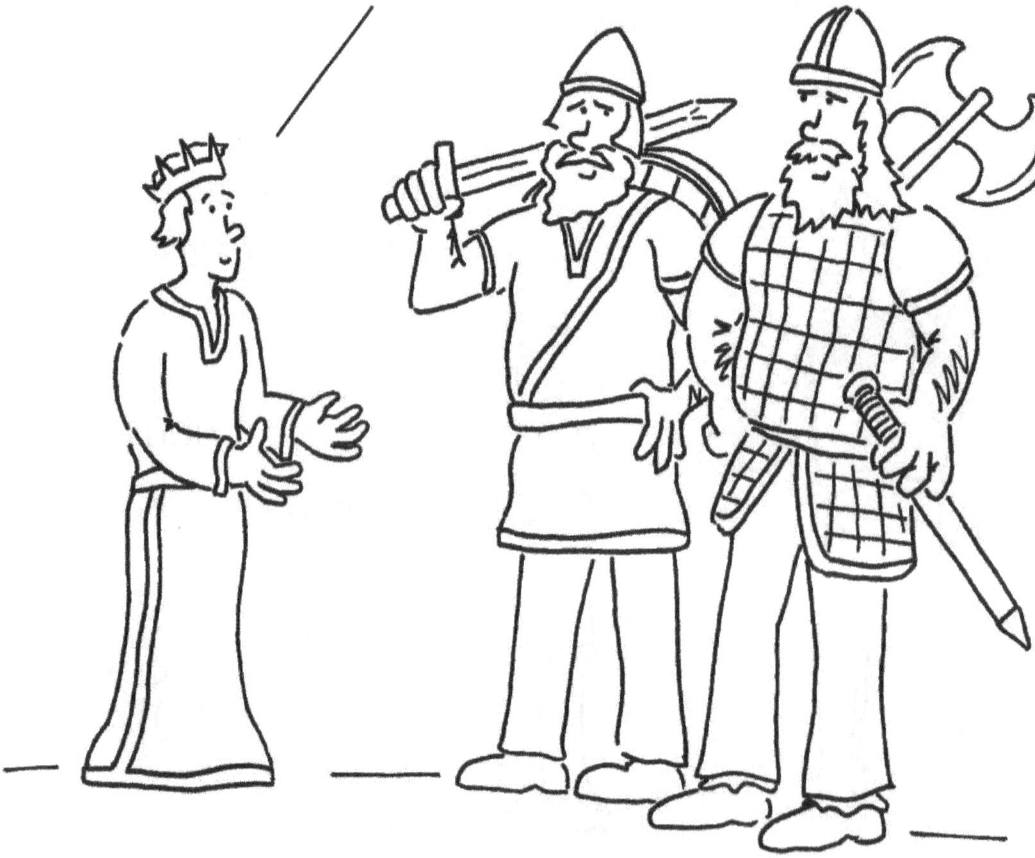

King Vortigern's well thought out plan

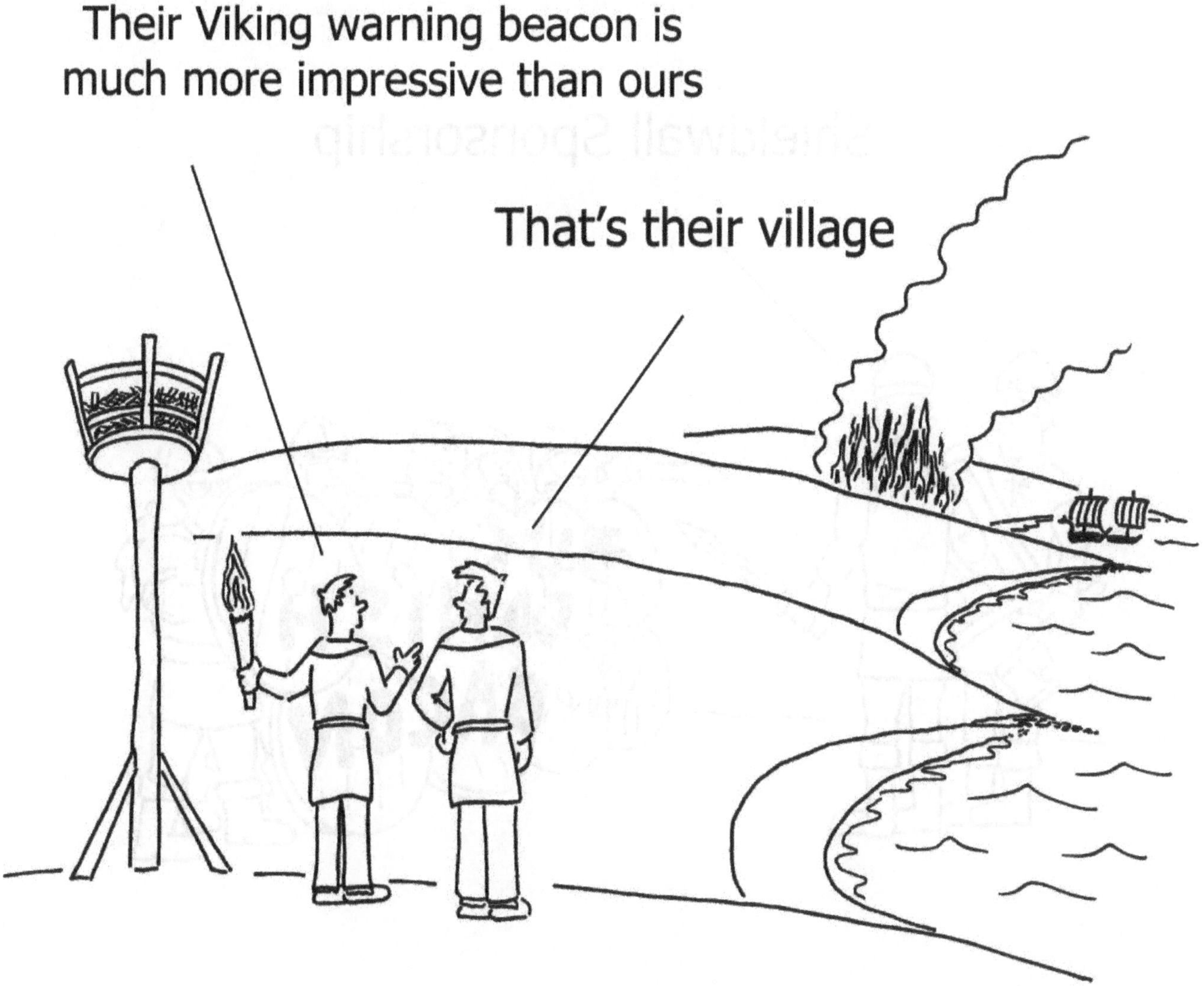
Their Viking warning beacon is much more impressive than ours
That's their village

Shieldwall Sponsorship

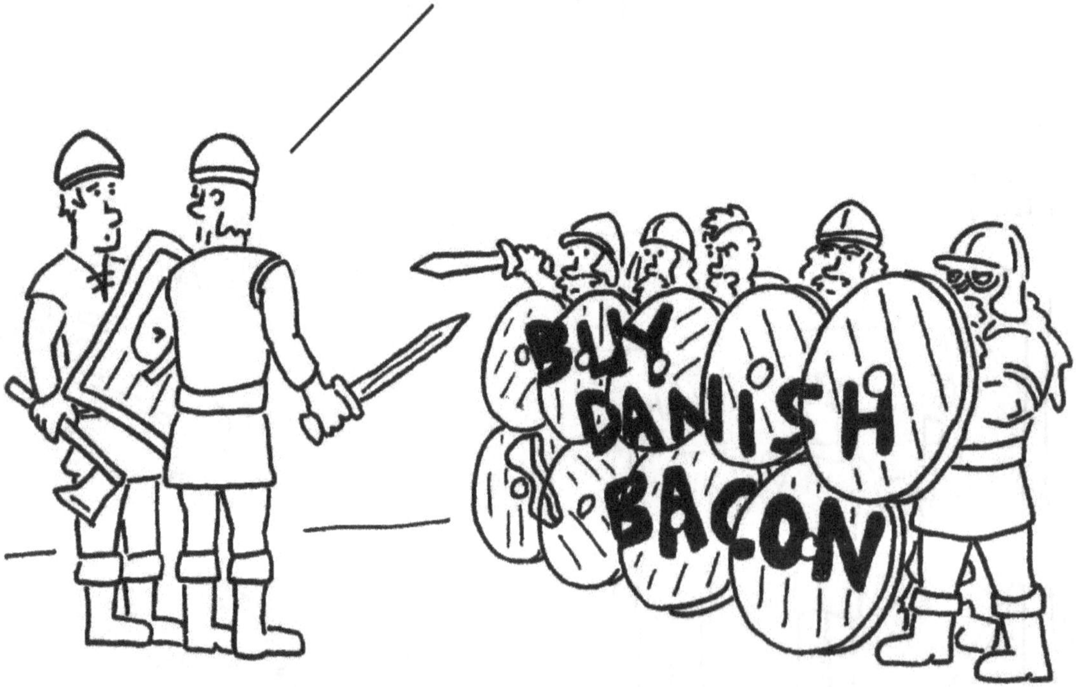
BUY DANISH BACON

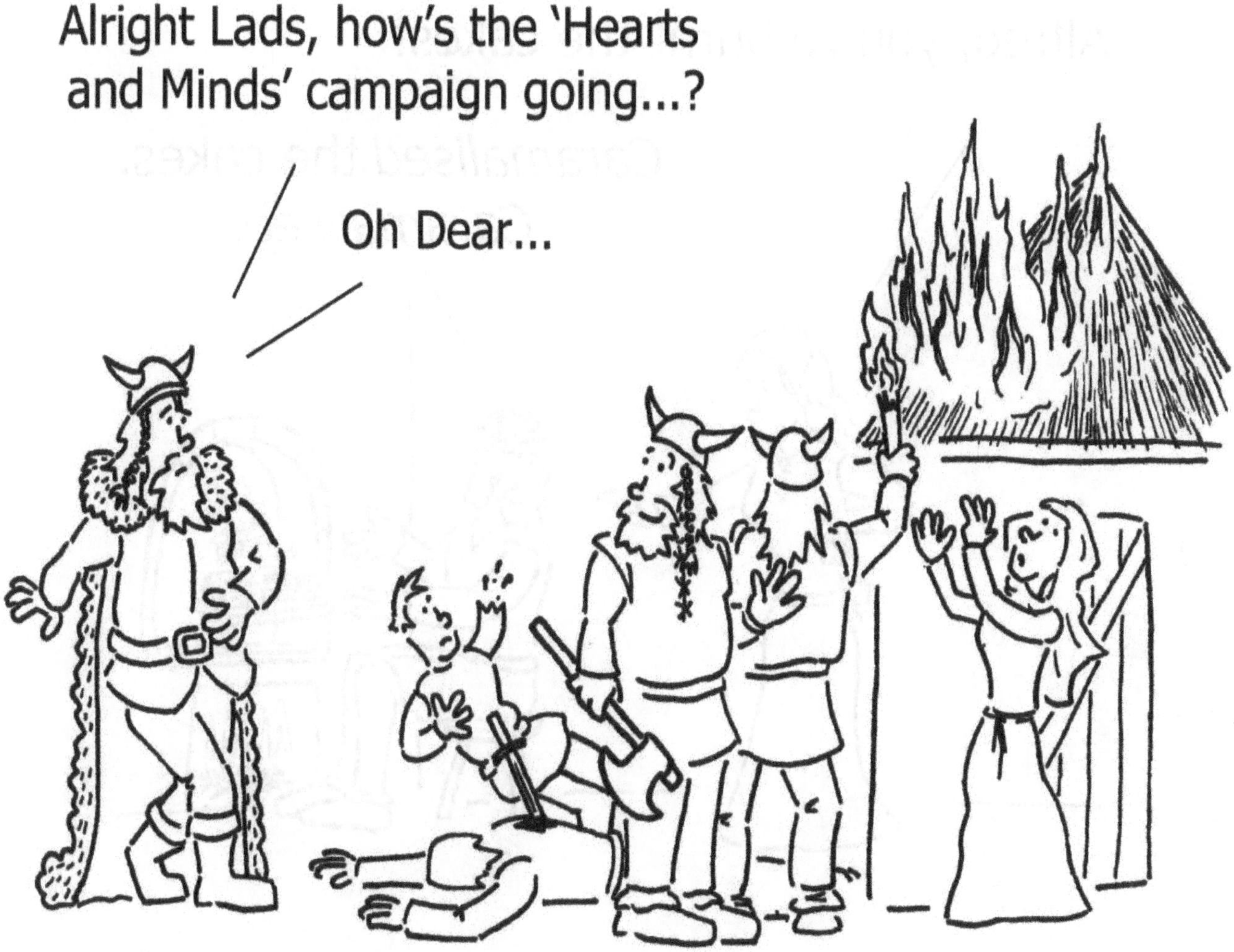
Alright Lads, how's the 'Hearts and Minds' campaign going...?
Oh Dear...

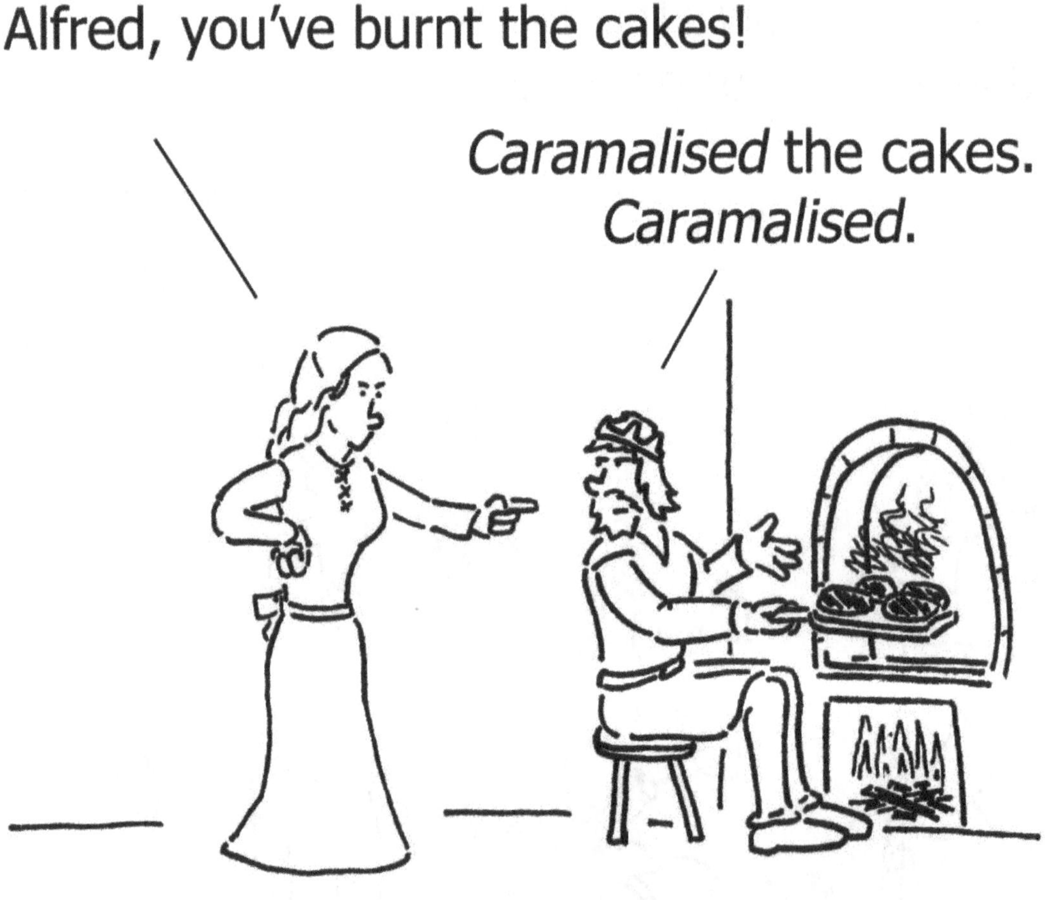
Alfred, you've burnt the cakes!
Caramalised the cakes. *Caramalised*.

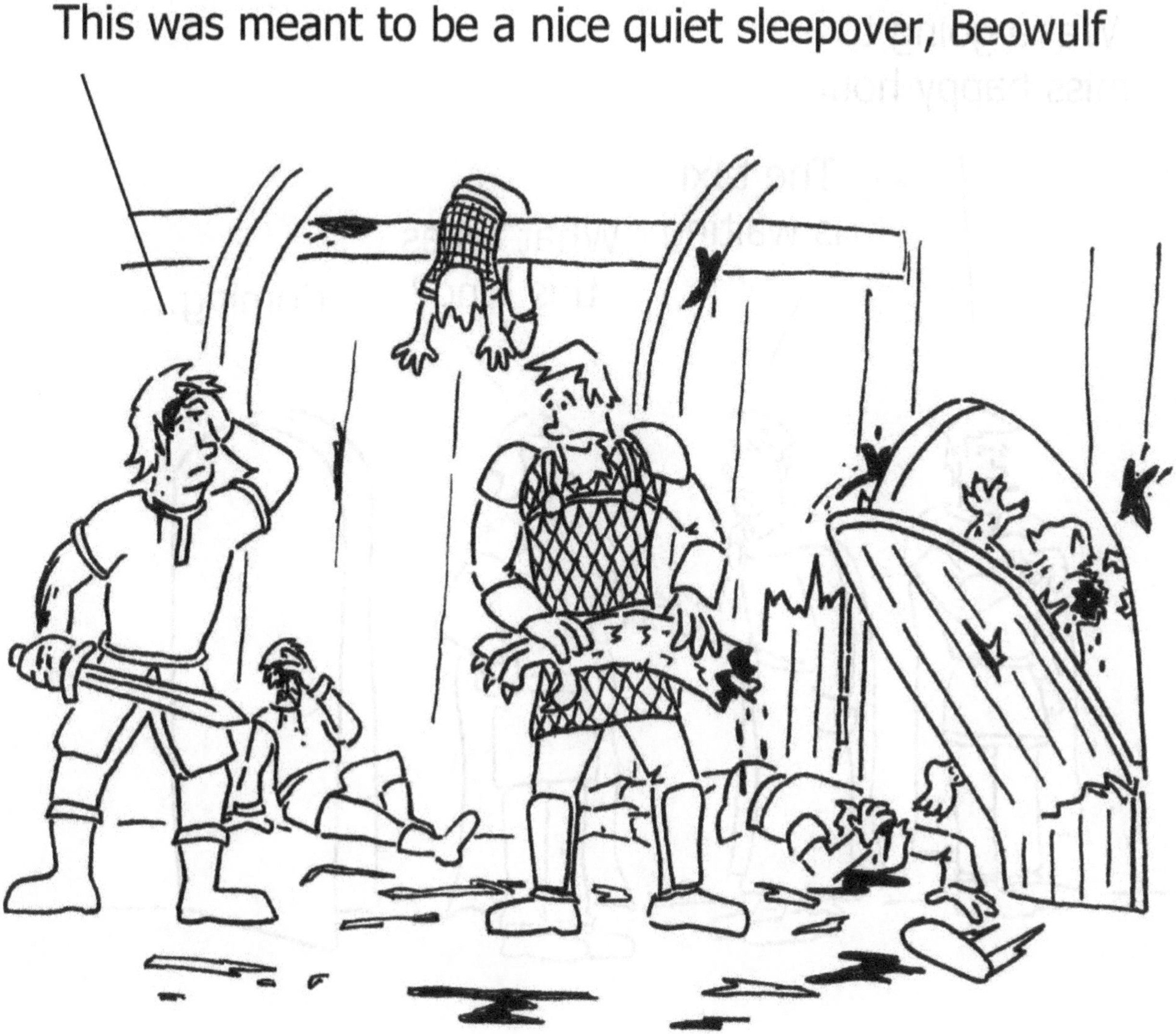
This was meant to be a nice quiet sleepover, Beowulf

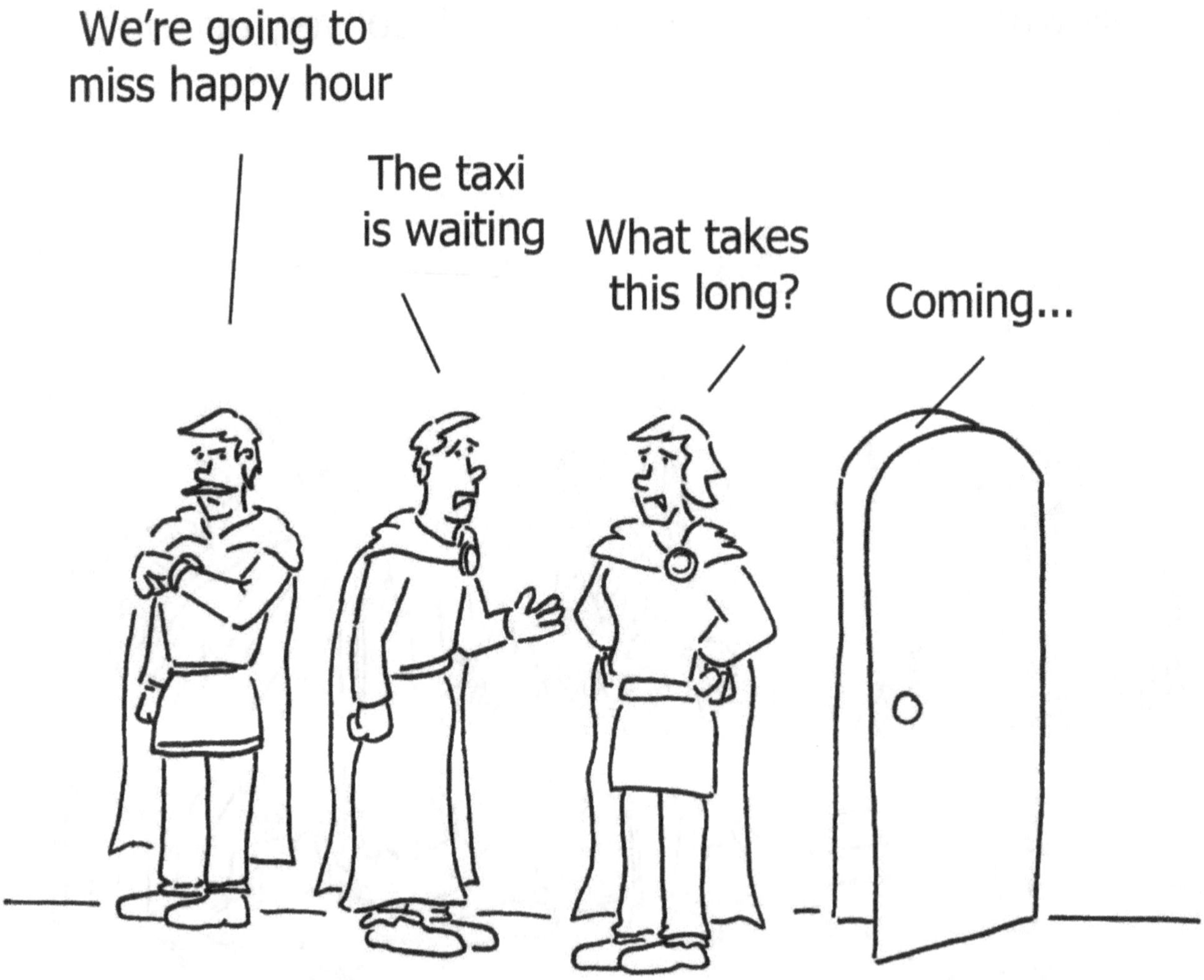
We're going to miss happy hour
The taxi is waiting
What takes this long?
Coming...

Ethelred the Unready

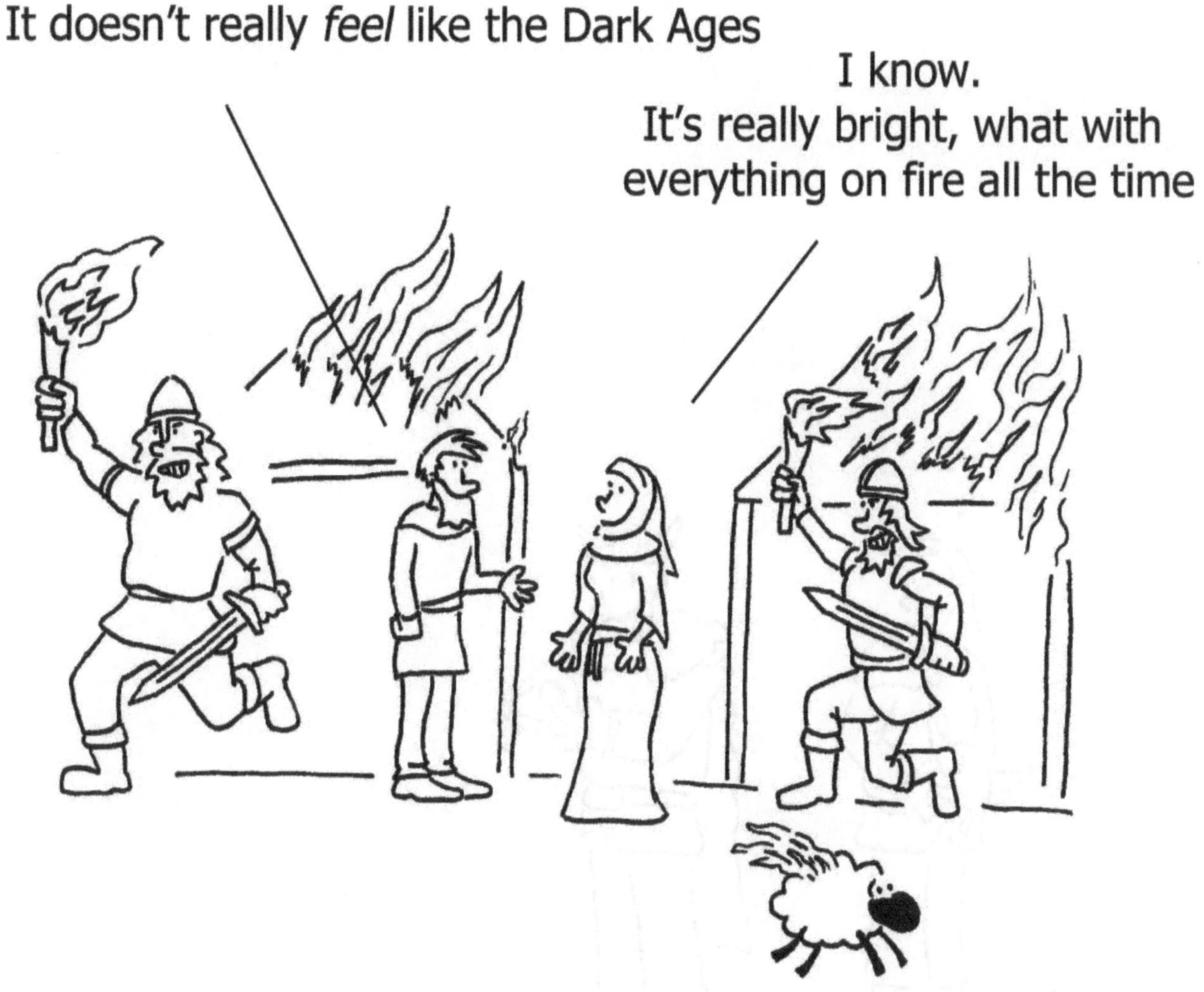
It doesn't really *feel* like the Dark Ages
I know.
It's really bright, what with everything on fire all the time

The Norman Conquest

After the raids, invasions and upheavals of the Dark Ages, the people of Britain could have done with a break. What they actually got was a cataclysm. Even to people familiar with incursion, this was a whole new experience with an impact more akin to a 1950's alien invasion story.

Once the T's had been crossed and the eyes had been arrowed on the Bayeux Tapestry, the Normans embarked upon a wholesale shake-up. Most of the English ruling class had been wiped out at Hastings, which made the reorganisation more straightforward for the newcomers.

Castles transformed the landscape, French became the language of state and the people found themselves listed, reviewed and taxed thanks to the Doomsday Survey (the book of which became the bestseller of 1086).

None of this change was achieved through polite suggestion. This was social change at sword-point and the North of England had a particularly rough time of it. Still, this was just teething pain and the Kingdom would grow up to be secure and successful – right?
Not really. William the Conqueror's heirs didn't inherit his knack for staying alive. William Rufus' suspicious hunting accident and William Adelin's shipwreck led to a protracted period of civil war between cousins Stephen and Mathilda, known as 'The Anarchy'. Great.

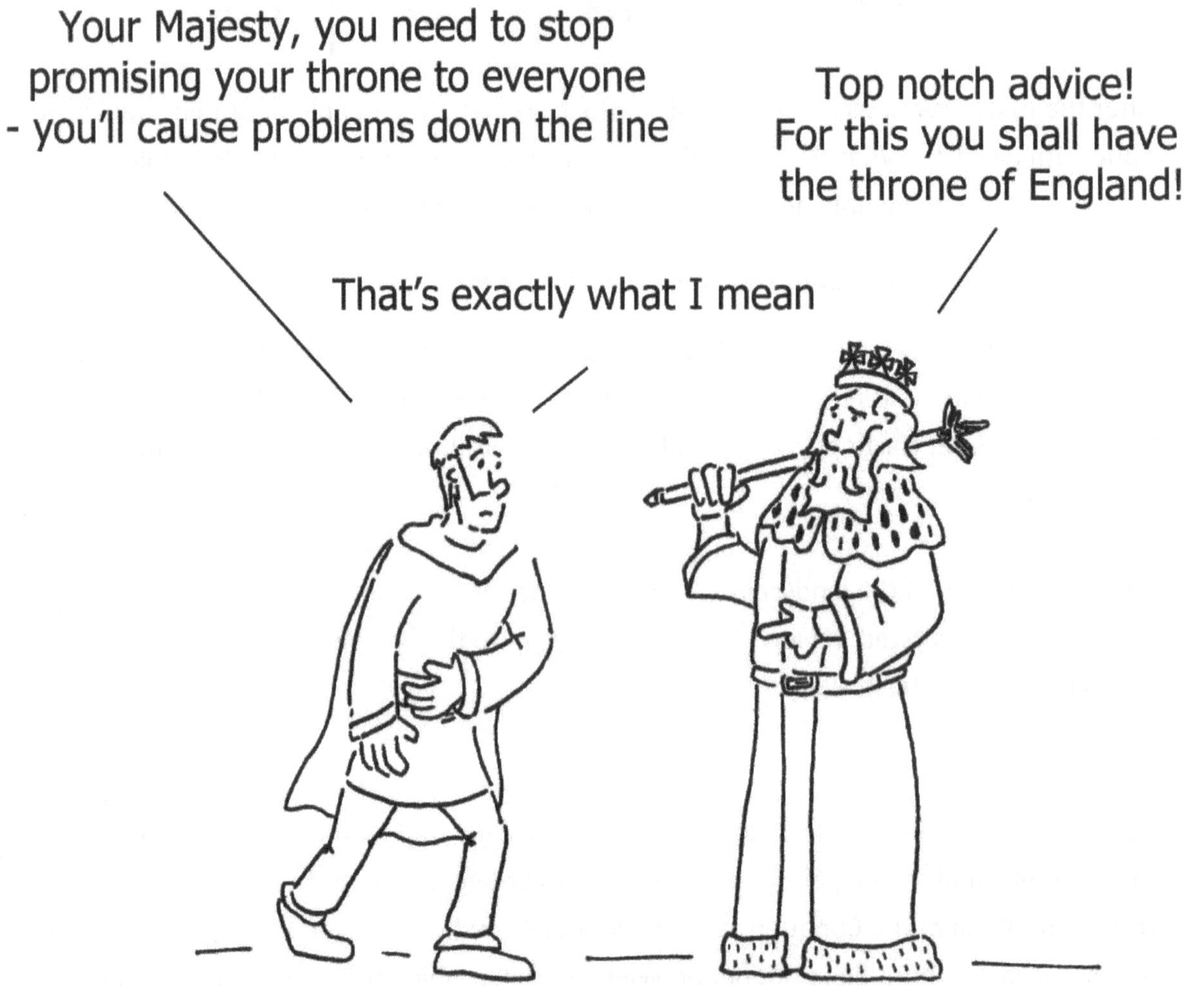
Your Majesty, you need to stop promising your throne to everyone - you'll cause problems down the line
Top notch advice! For this you shall have the throne of England!
That's exactly what I mean

The court of Edward the Confessor

And that's the last of you!
1066 will for ever be remembered as the year Harold Godwinson
rid England of the Vikings for good at Stamford Bridge

well...
unless anything
else happens...

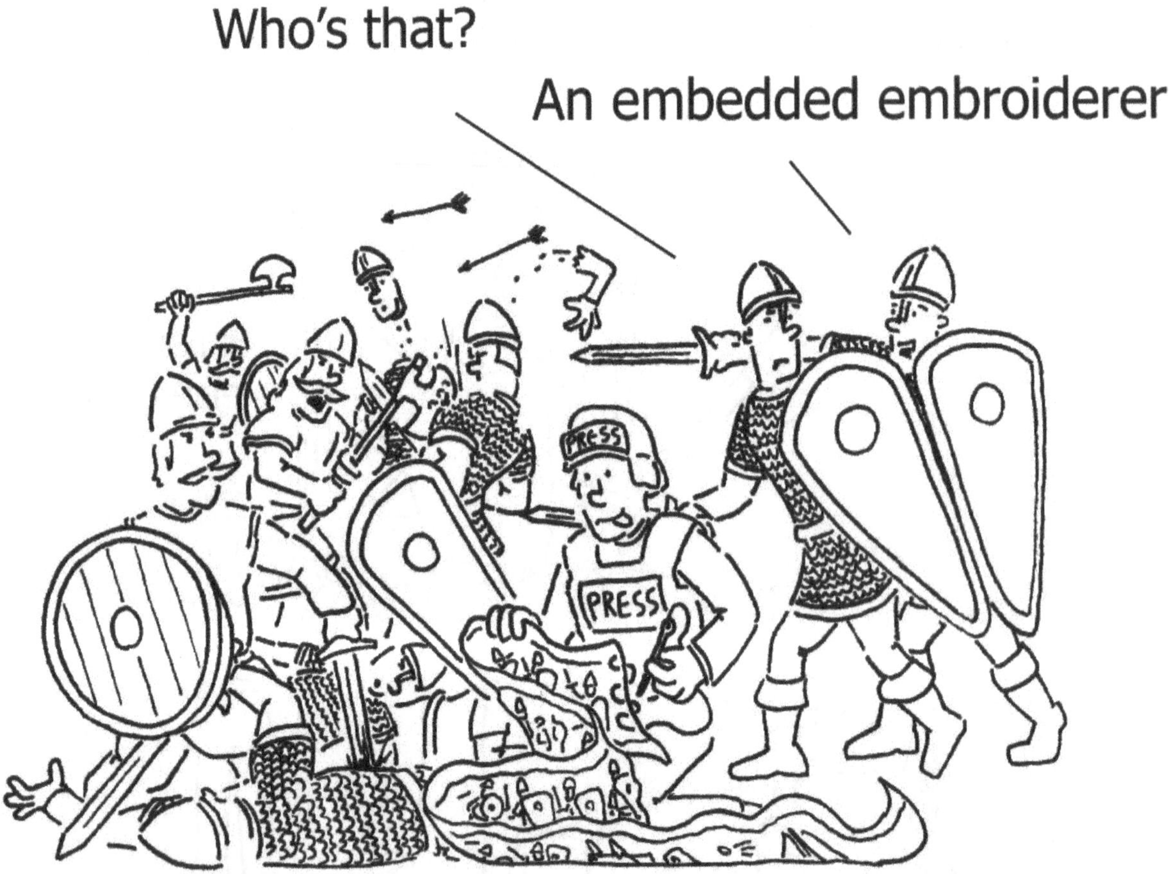
Who's that?
An embedded embroiderer
PRESS
PRESS

Hastings 1066

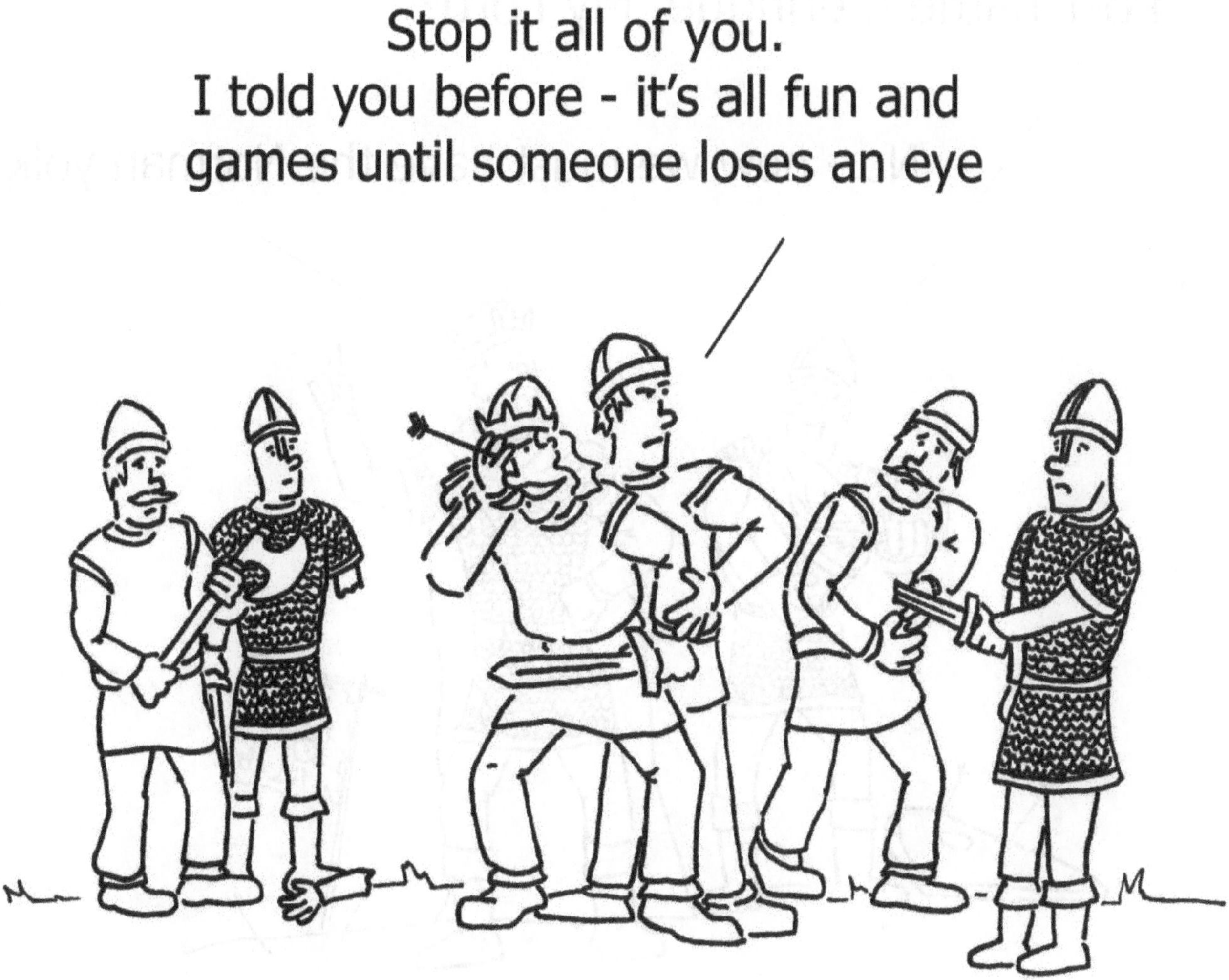
Stop it all of you.
I told you before - it's all fun and games until someone loses an eye

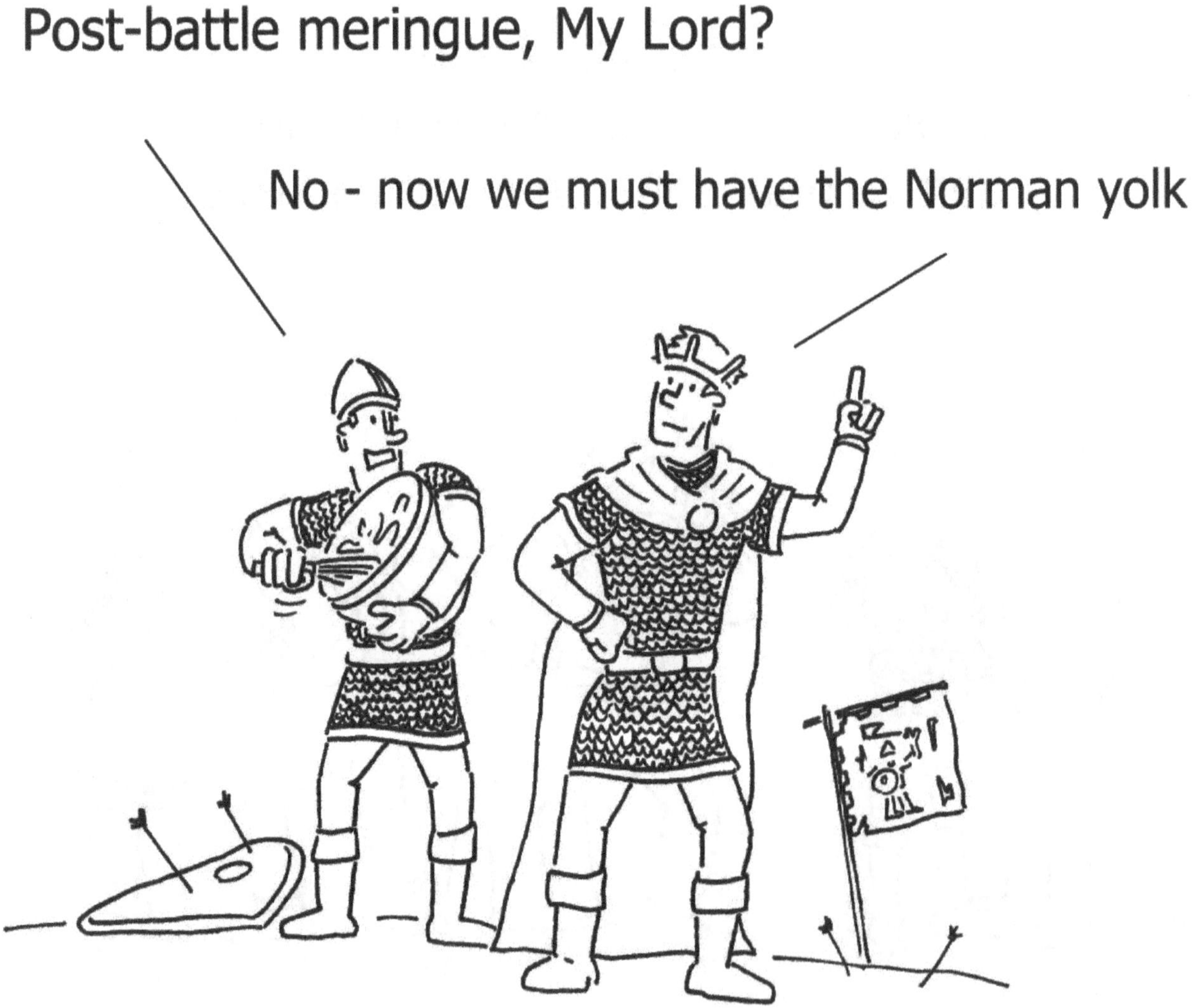
Post-battle meringue, My Lord?
No - now we must have the Norman yolk

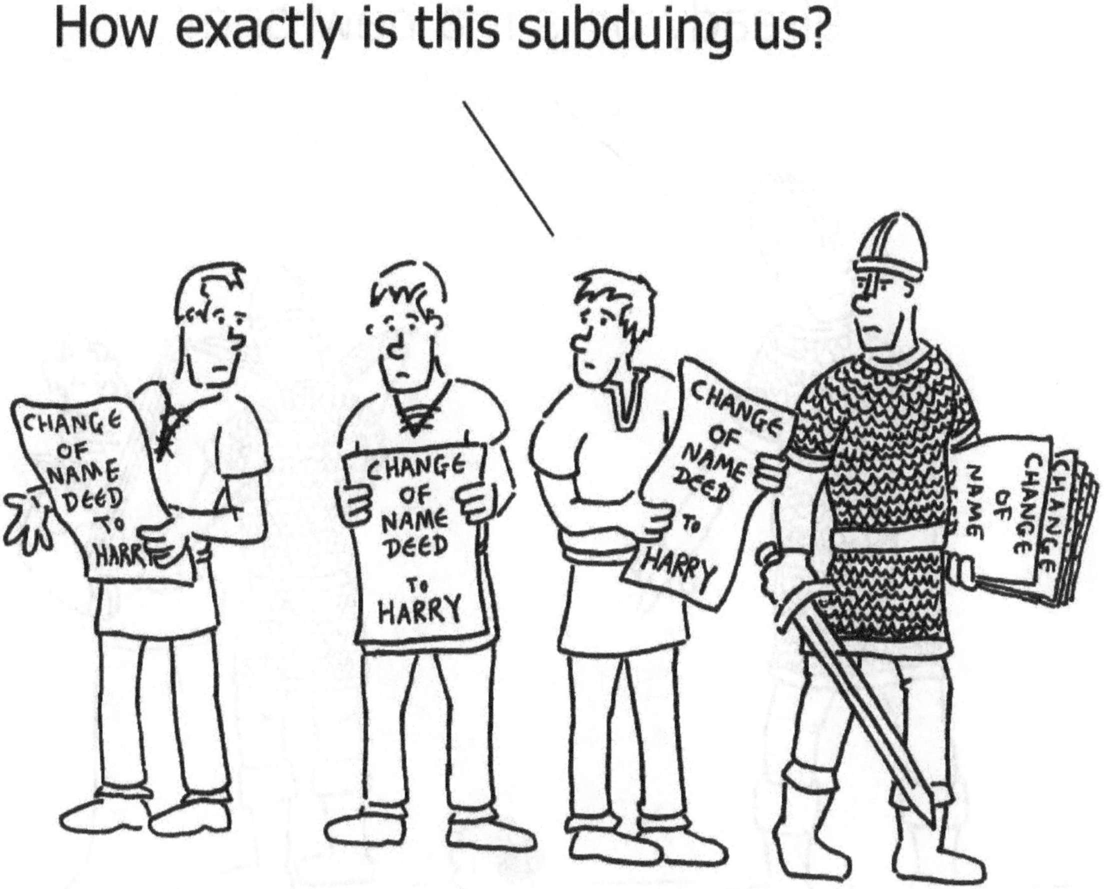
How exactly is this subduing us?
CHANGE OF NAME DEED TO HARRY
CHANGE OF NAME DEED TO HARRY
CHANGE OF NAME DEED TO HARRY
CHANGE OF NAME

The Harrying of The North

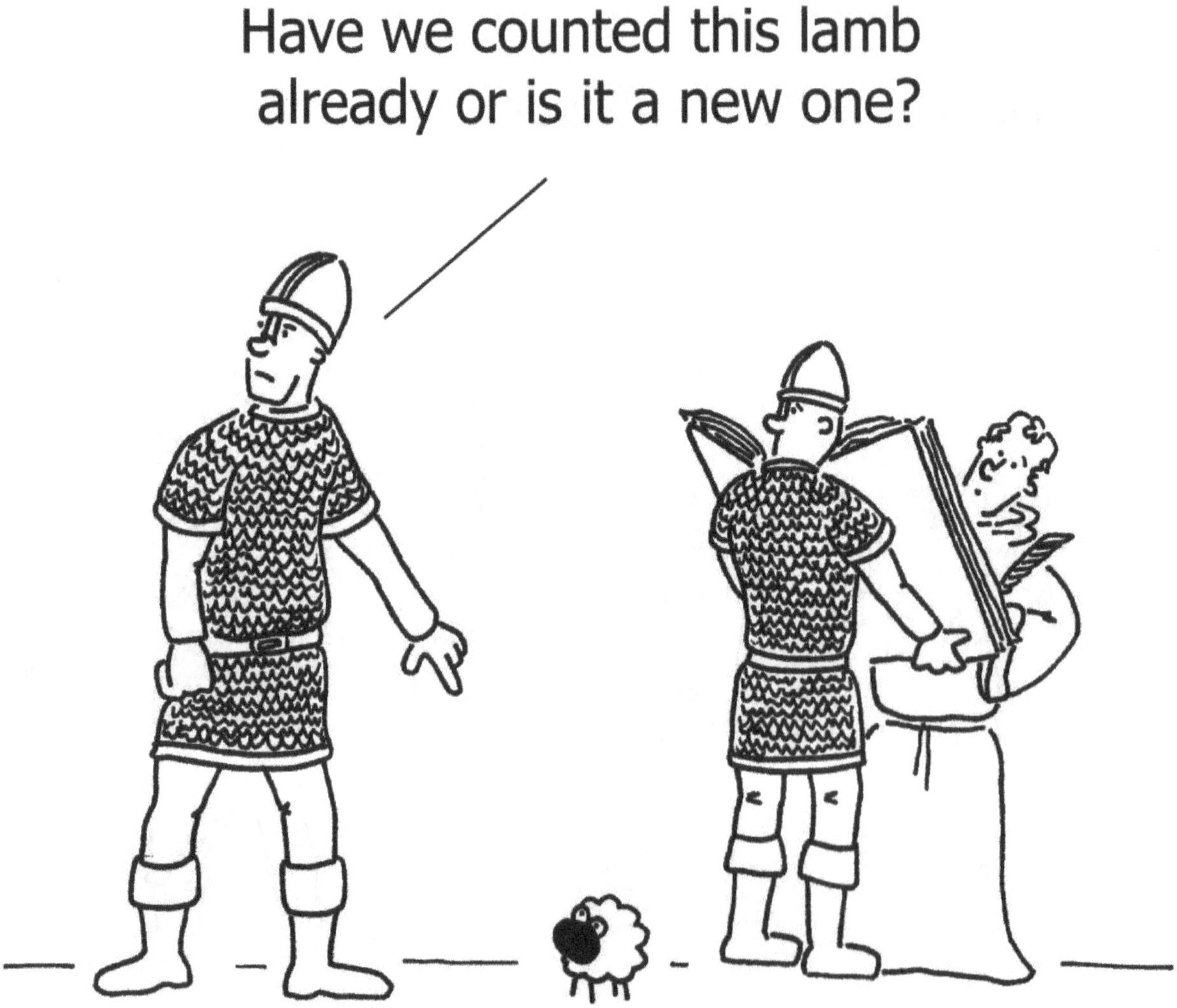
Have we counted this lamb already or is it a new one?

The Doomsday Survey faced livestock registration problems in the spring

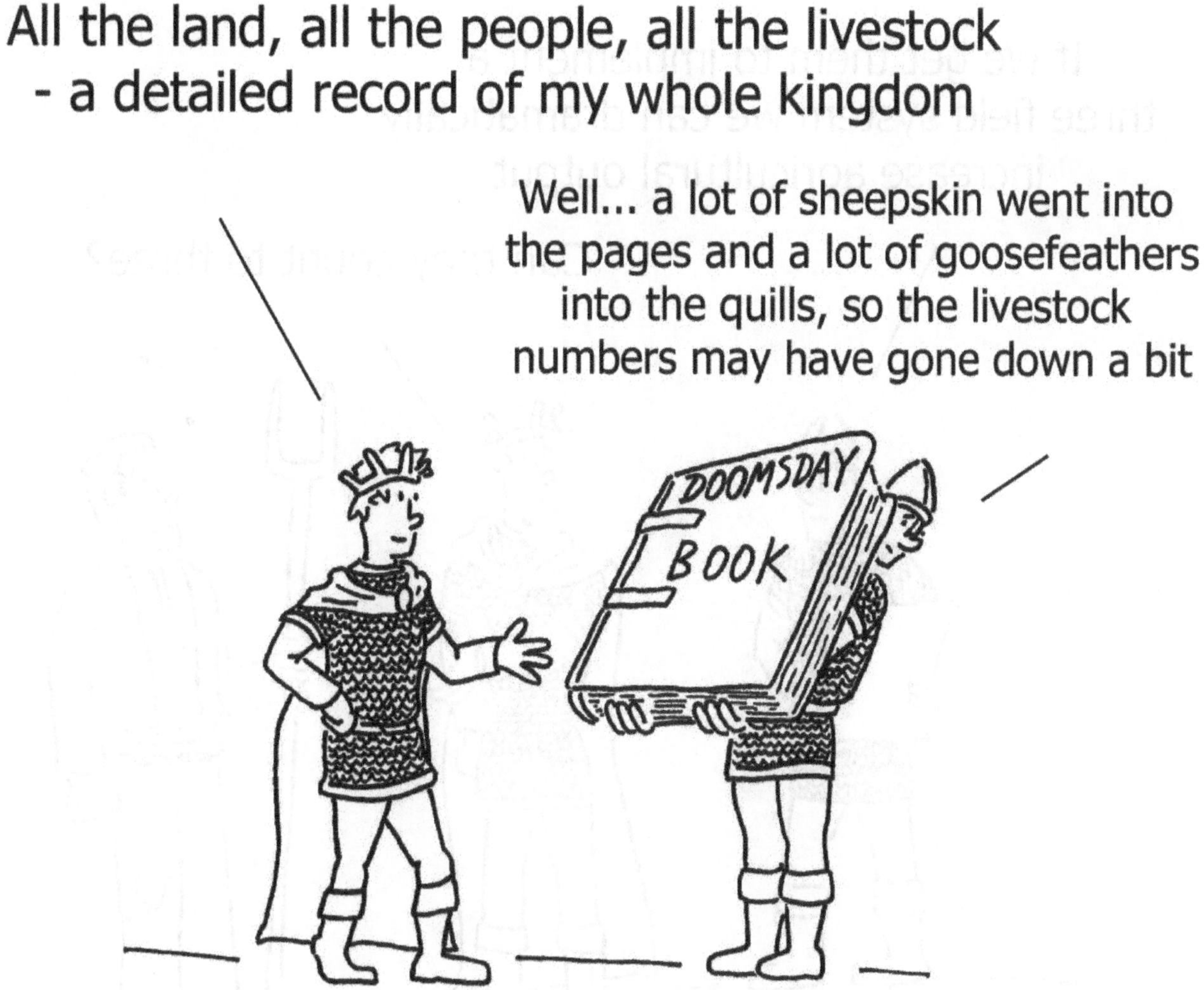
All the land, all the people, all the livestock - a detailed record of my whole kingdom
Well... a lot of sheepskin went into the pages and a lot of goosefeathers into the quills, so the livestock numbers may have gone down a bit
DOOMSDAY BOOK

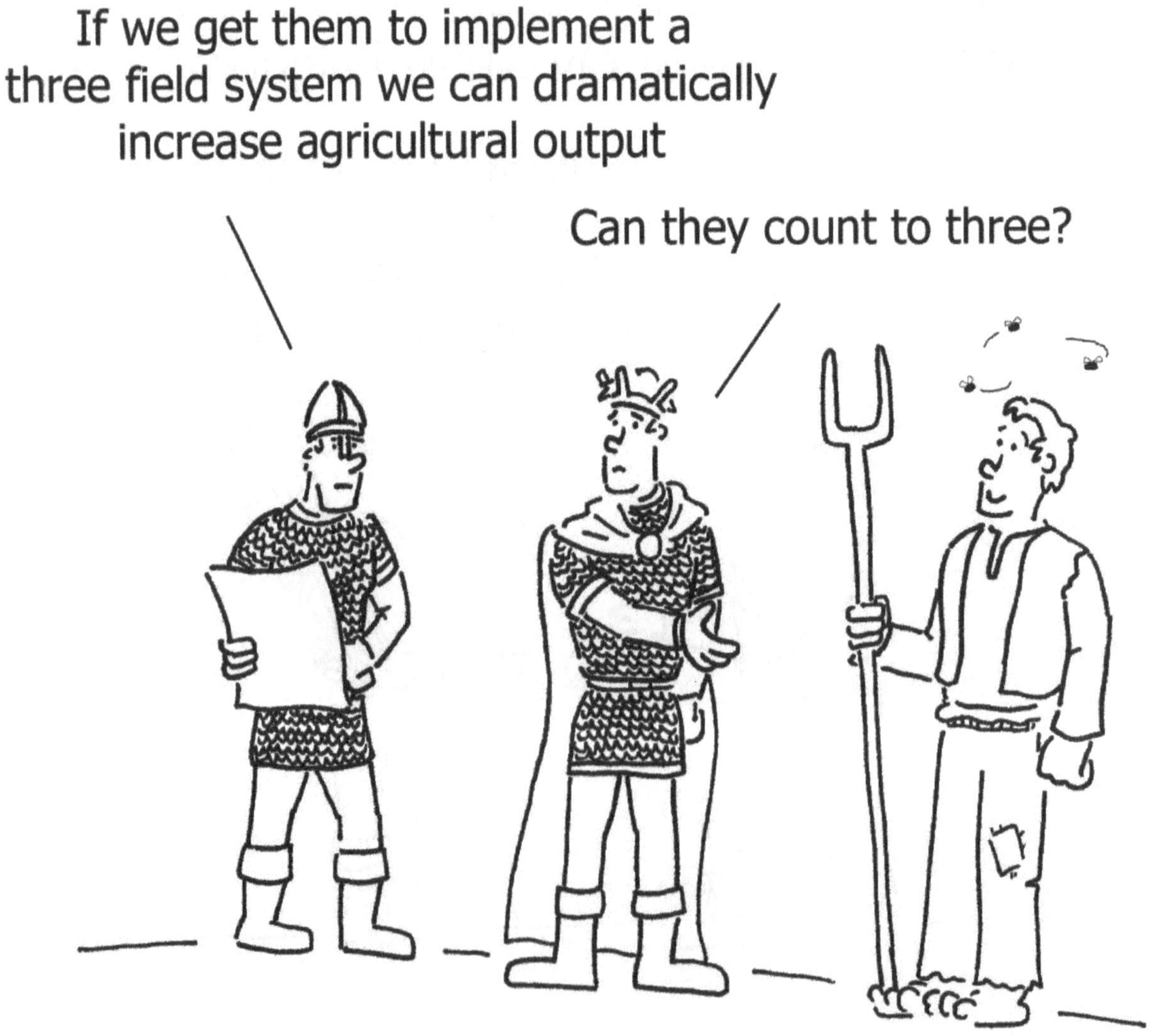
If we get them to implement a three field system we can dramatically increase agricultural output
Can they count to three?

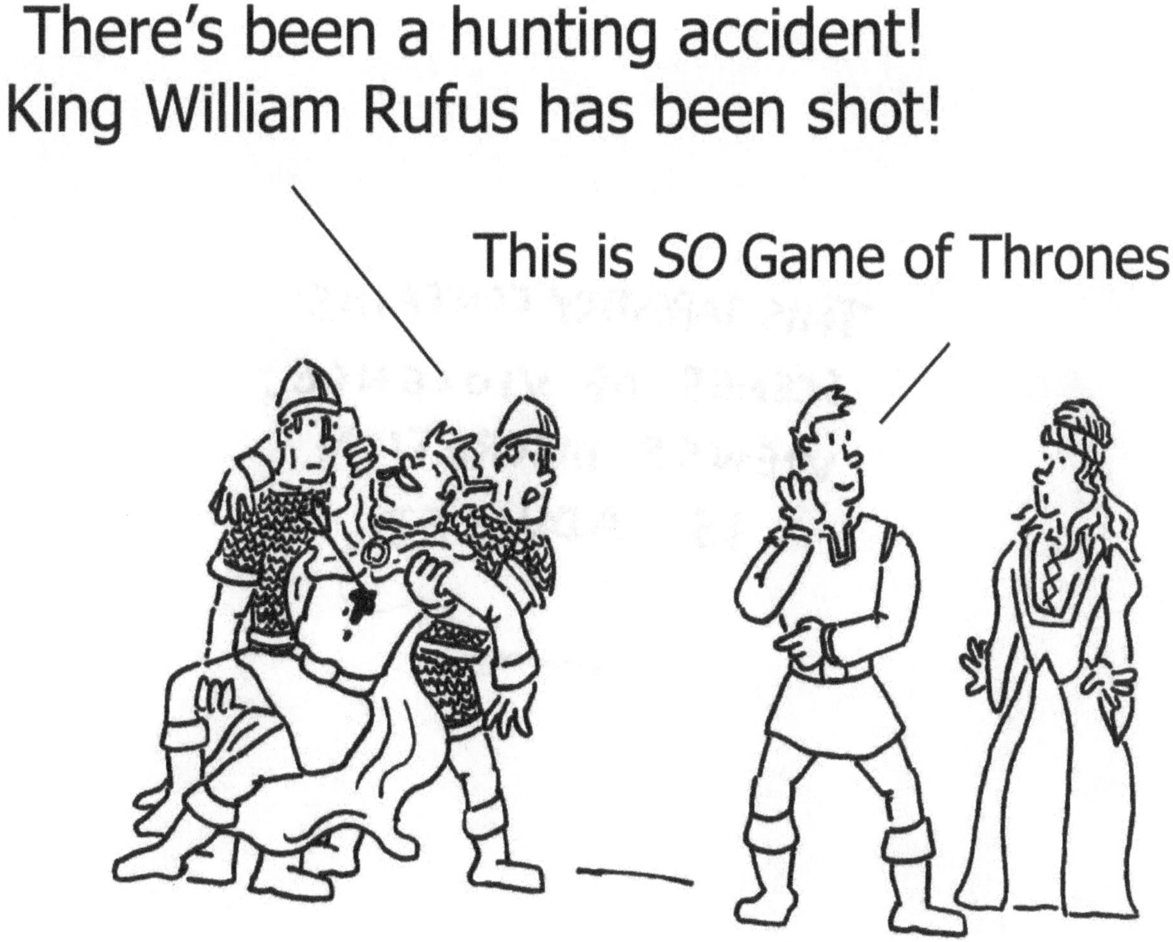
There's been a hunting accident!
King William Rufus has been shot!
This is *SO* Game of Thrones

THIS TAPESTRY CONTAINS
SCENES OF VIOLENCE.
VIEWER DISCRETION
IS ADVISED.

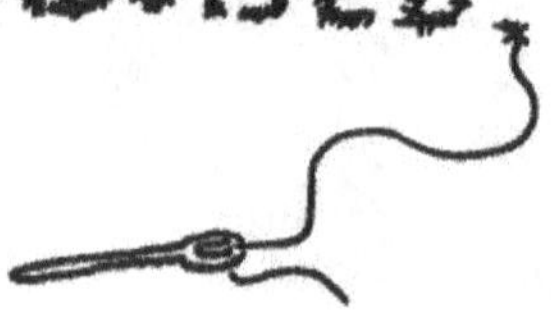

The Middle Ages

The title 'Dark Ages' has already been taken, which is a shame because this next period in Britain's history would have been a good contender for the title 'Dark'. War, famine, plague and death are ever-present characters here – though there's a particularly lengthy Hundred Years' War and a particularly virulent Black Death.

The series of wars between England and France (which came to be known as the Hundred Years' War) is slightly complicated. The English crown ruled large parts of what we now know as France, so 'the French' often fought 'the French'. Also the nobility on both sides spoke French and had more in common with each other than the ordinary folk of either country.

All looked to be done and dusted by 1420 and the Treaty of Troyes which, on the death of the French King would leave Henry V (fresh from his victory at Agincourt) as King of England and France.

All Henry had to do was stay alive, but this was the Middle Ages and death was round the corner for everyone. Dysentery achieved what the French army could not and with Henry gone, the whole business kicked off again.

Of course, many believed the treaty still to be valid and so English kings were crowned as King of England and France until George III dropped the title in 1801. Very gracious of him.

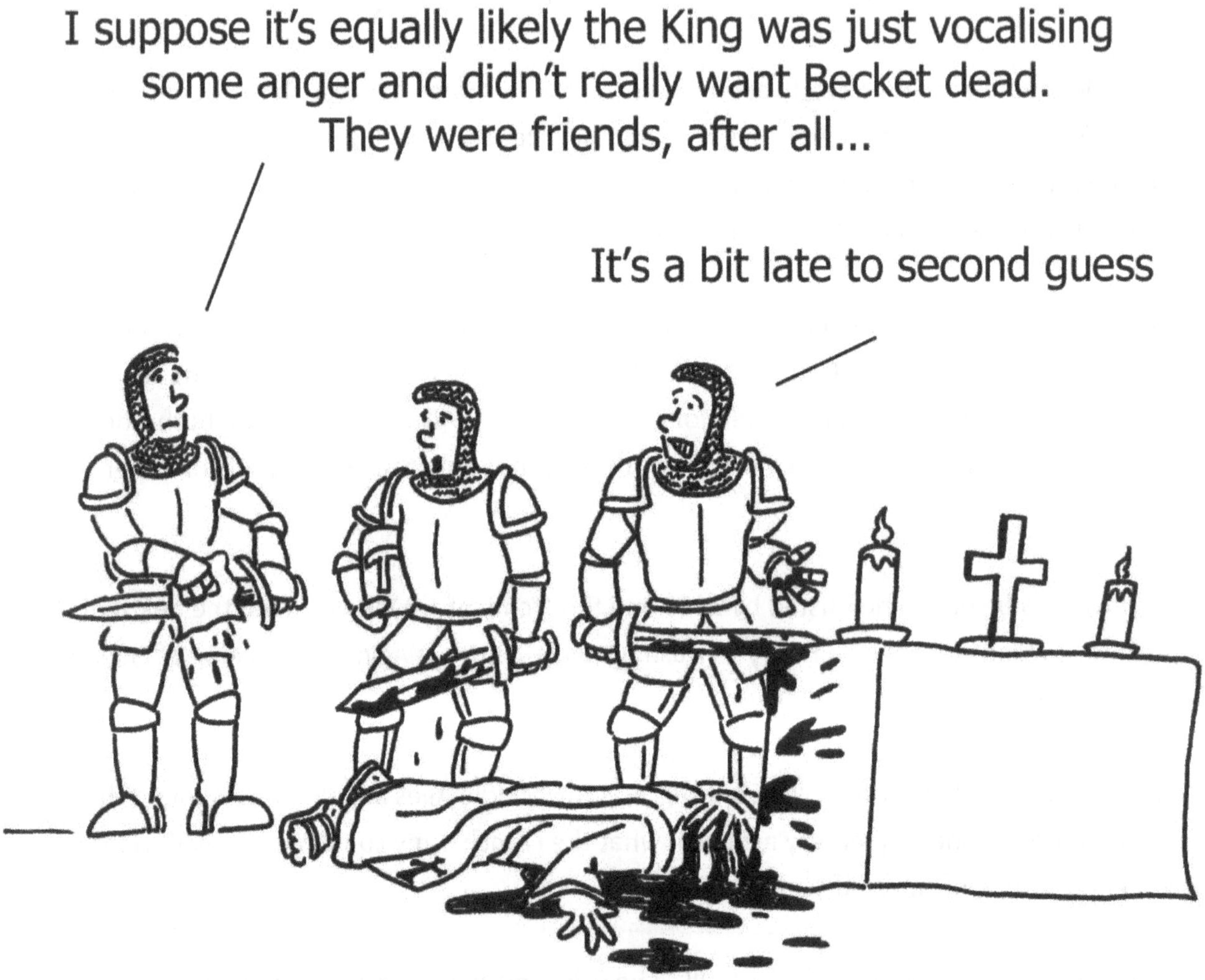
I suppose it's equally likely the King was just vocalising some anger and didn't really want Becket dead. They were friends, after all...
It's a bit late to second guess

Canterbury Catherdral, December 29th 1170

OK, OK. you also have the right to watch Japanese cartoons...

Manga Carta

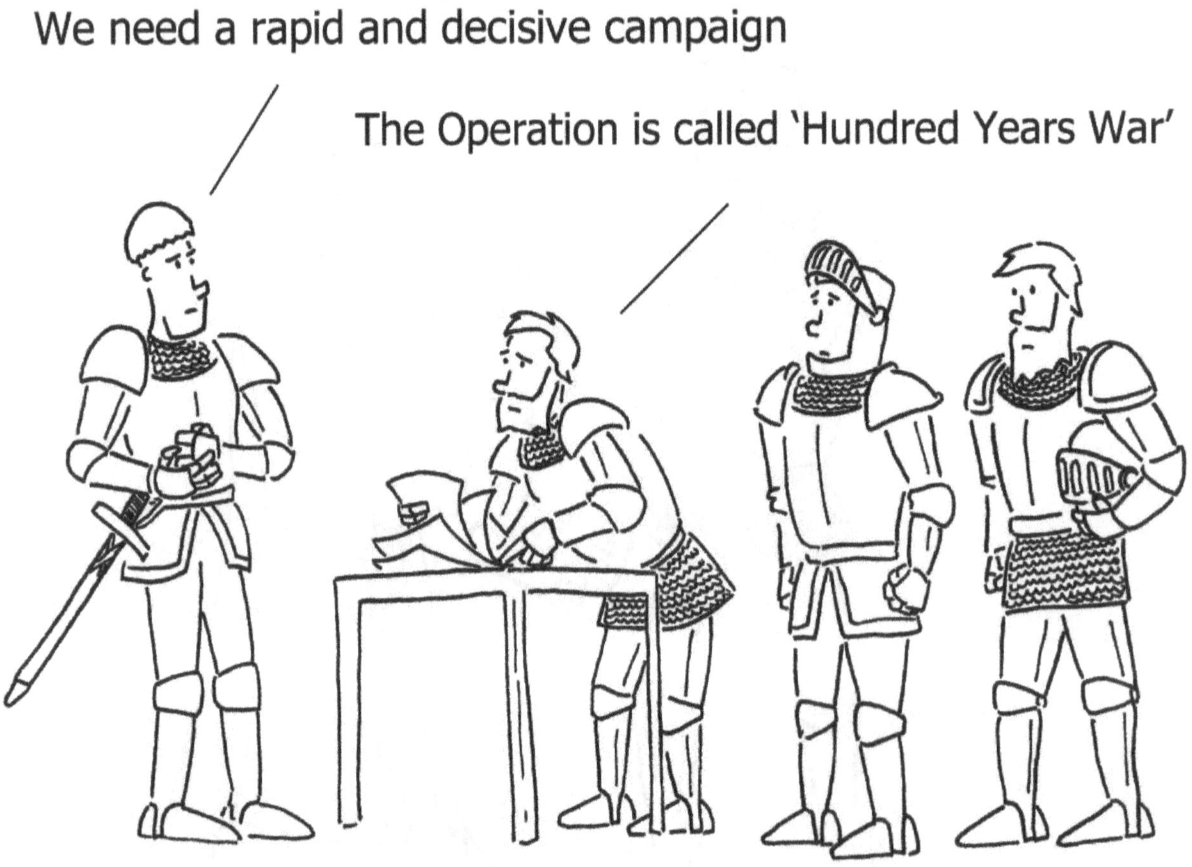
We need a rapid and decisive campaign
The Operation is called 'Hundred Years War'

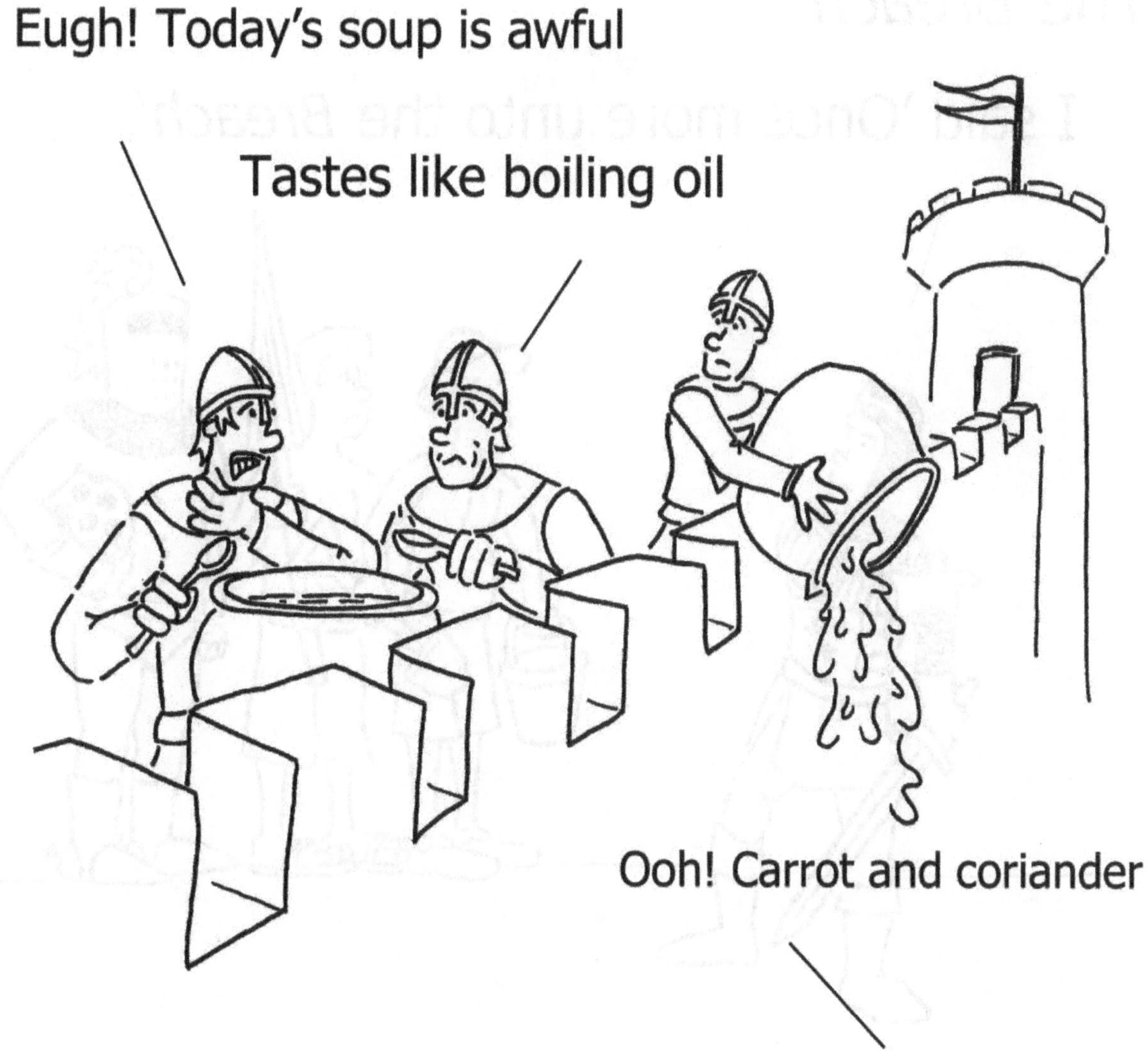
Eugh! Today's soup is awful
Tastes like boiling oil
Ooh! Carrot and coriander

The *Breach*

I said 'Once more unto the *Breach*'

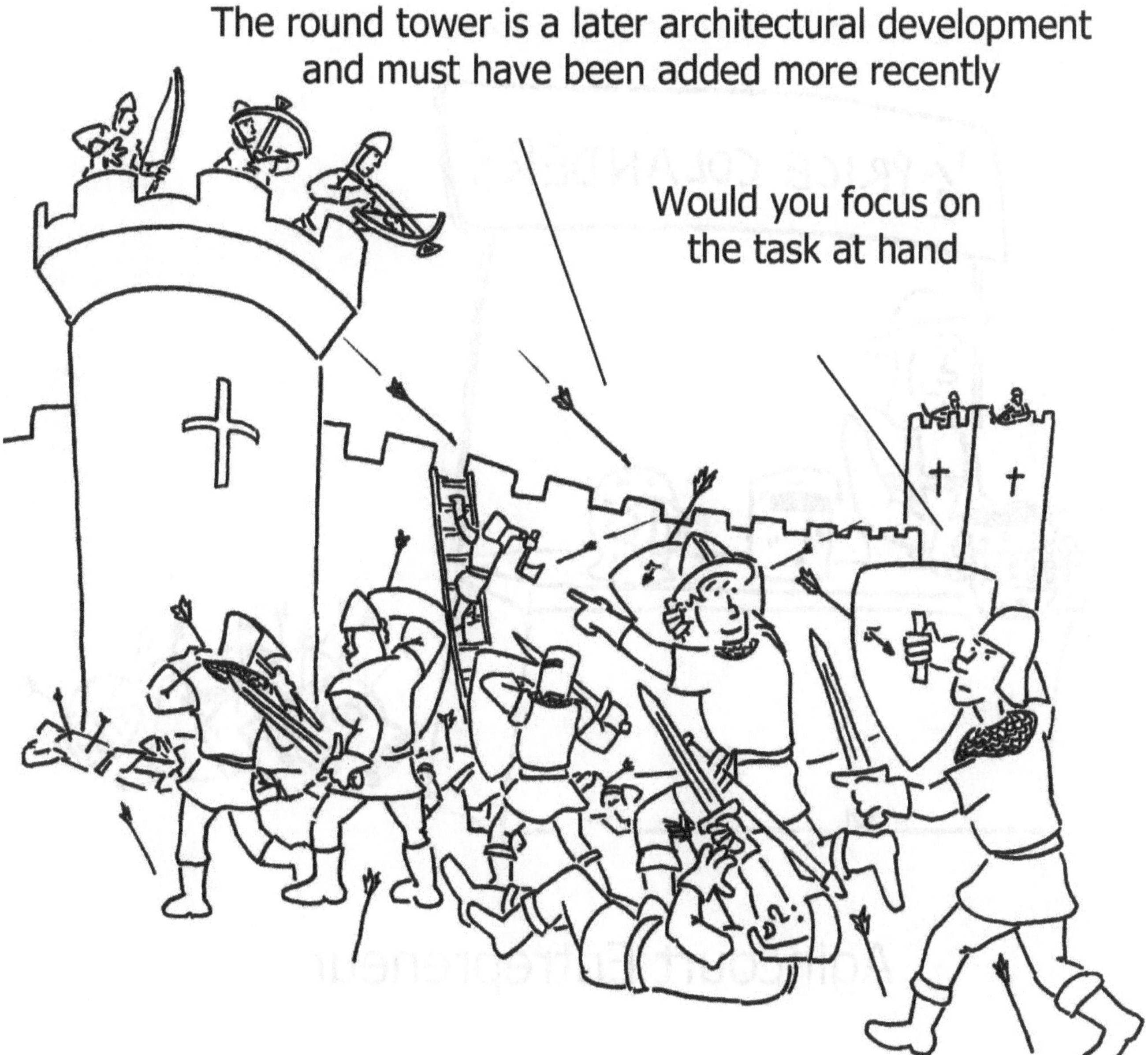
The round tower is a later architectural development and must have been added more recently
Would you focus on the task at hand

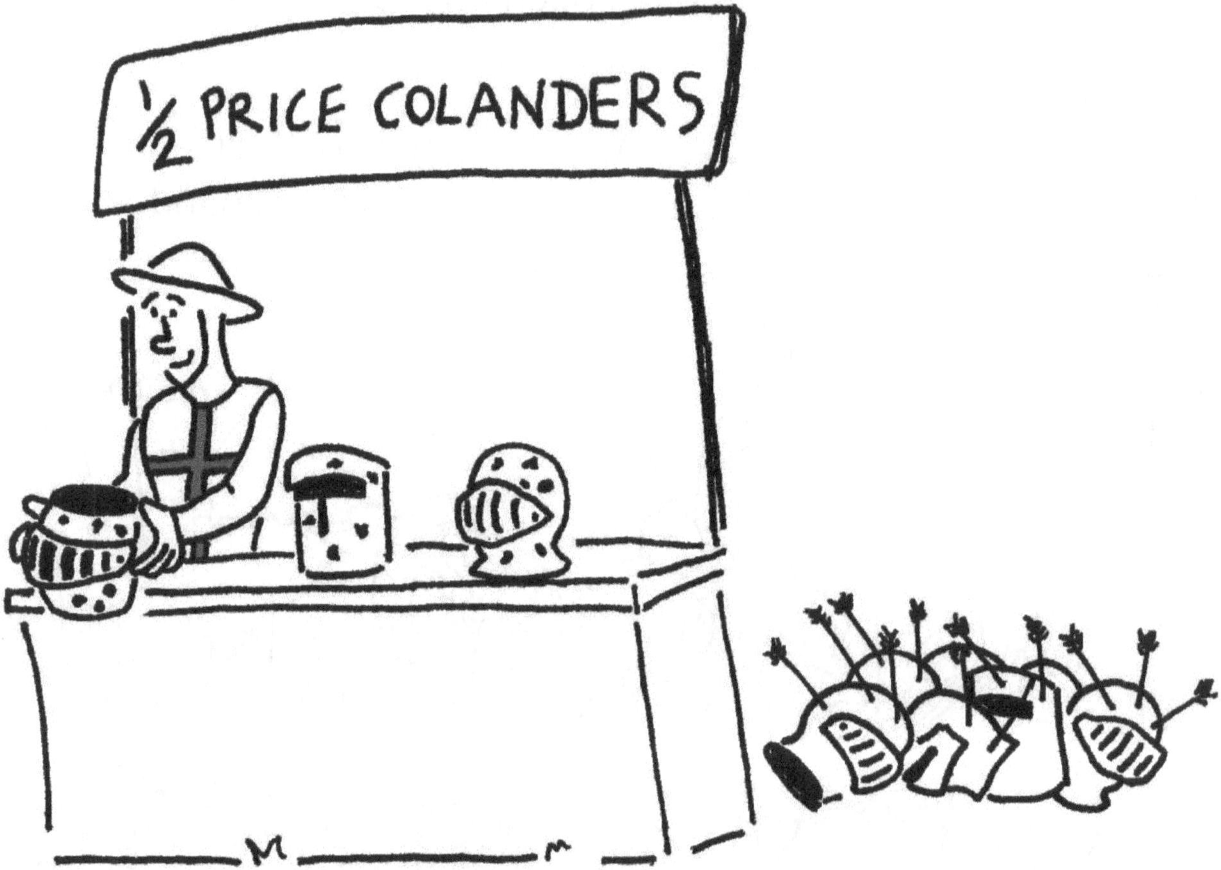
½ PRICE COLANDERS

Agincourt Entrepreneur

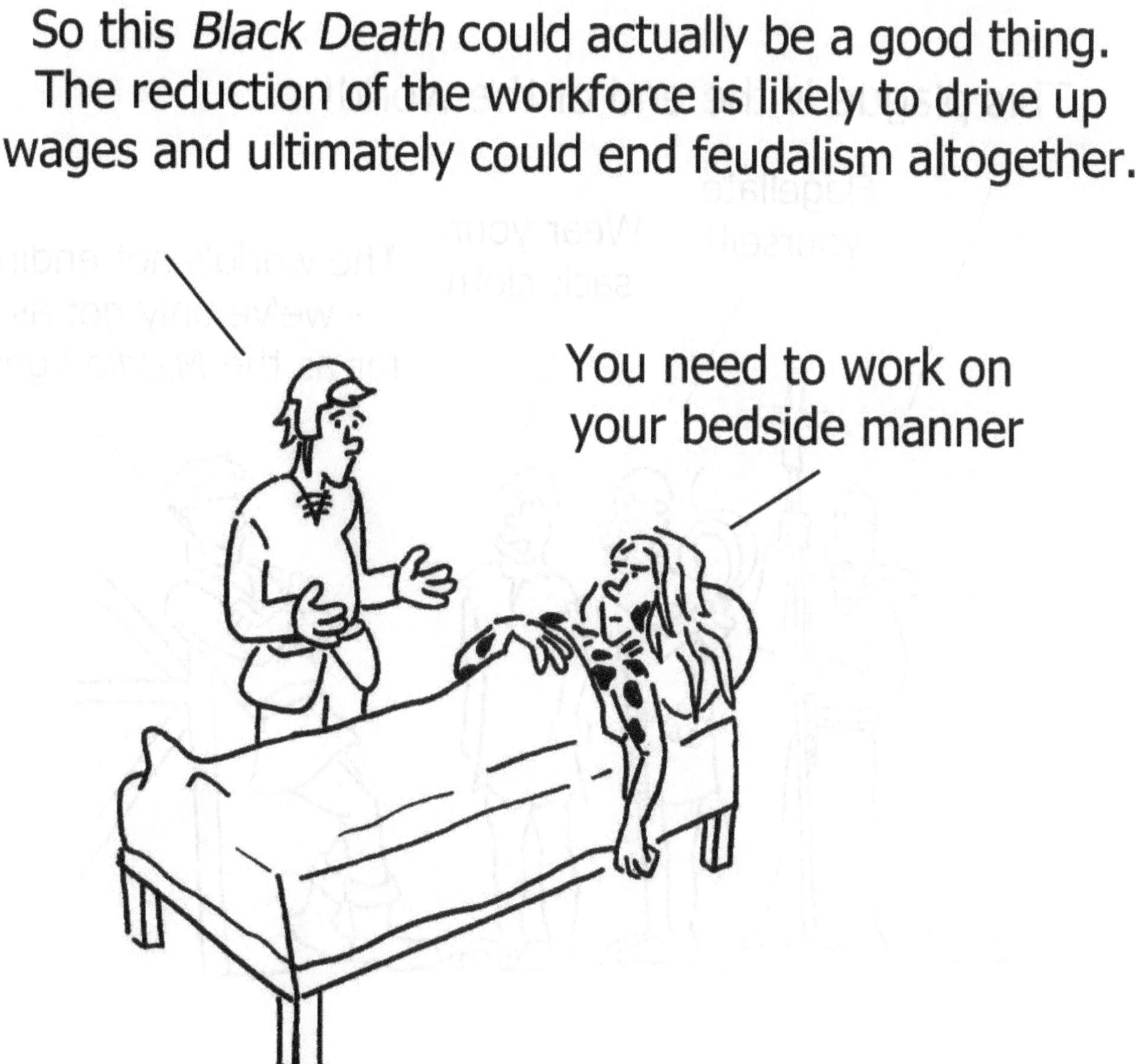
So this *Black Death* could actually be a good thing. The reduction of the workforce is likely to drive up wages and ultimately could end feudalism altogether.
You need to work on your bedside manner

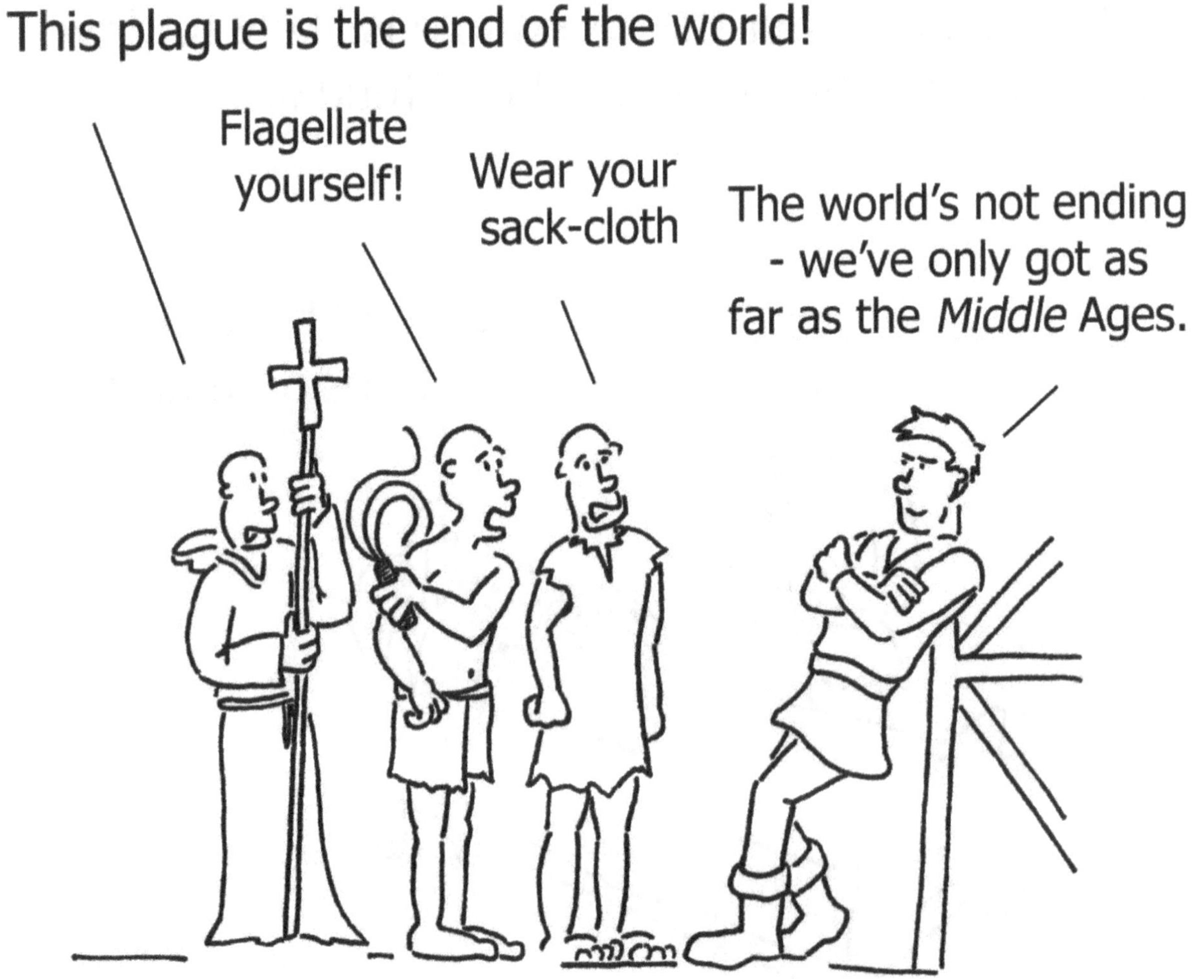
This plague is the end of the world!
Flagellate yourself!
Wear your sack-cloth
The world's not ending - we've only got as far as the *Middle* Ages.

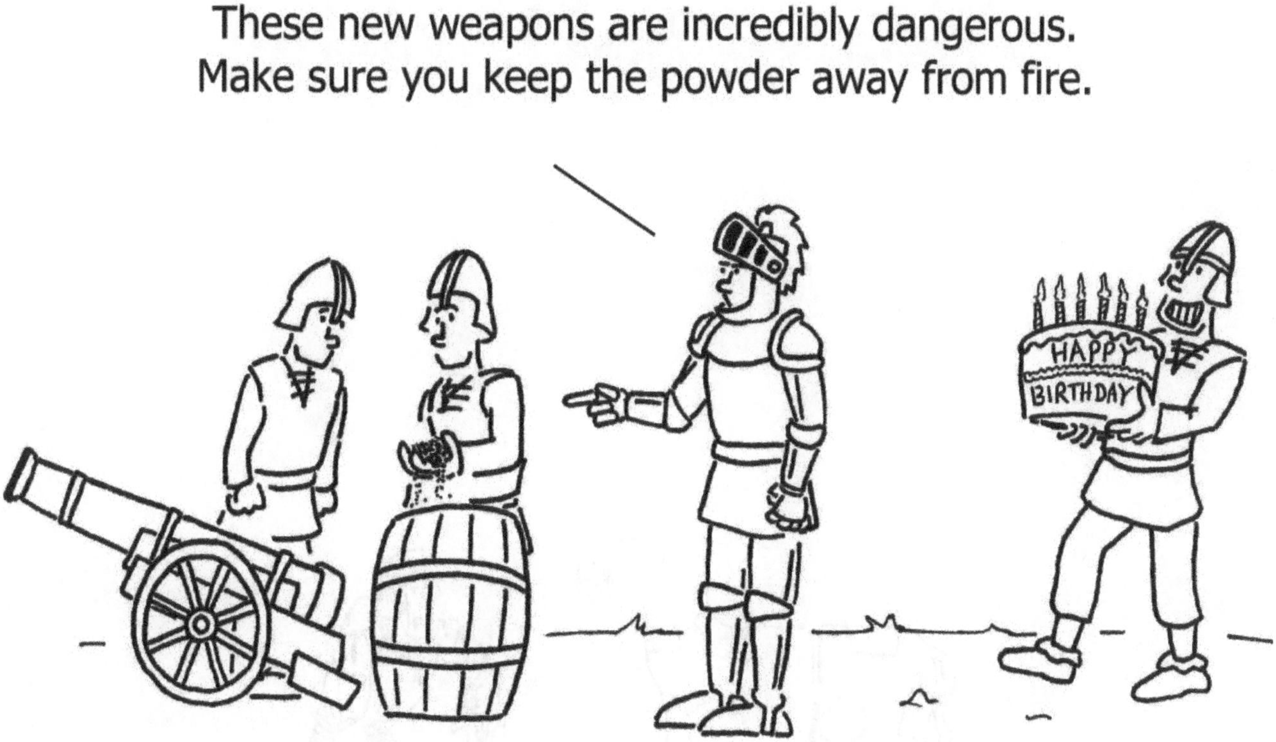
These new weapons are incredibly dangerous.
Make sure you keep the powder away from fire.
HAPPY
BIRTHDAY

The Tudors

The Middle Ages was bracketed by civil war. 'The Anarchy' marked the beginning and the Wars of the Roses concluded the period. Despite some last minute attempted horse trading, Richard III gave up the crown and his life at Bosworth Field and the Tudors emerged victorious.

Richard was buried in a Leicester car park and local legends said that if his bones were removed and reburied, Leicester City would win the Premiership title the following year*. When we think of the Tudors, we tend to think of Henry VIII. 'Divorced, beheaded, died, divorced, beheaded, survived' is the rhyme used to explain his 'fussy' approach to dating. The full rhyme begins 'Divorced, and in the process broke England's ties with Rome creating centuries of sectarian divide at home and fundamentally altering the nation's position in Europe...' There isn't space for the full rhyme.

The break from Rome was just one of the momentous events overseen by Tudor monarchs. In other news, the Spanish Armada was seen off by Drake (with a little help from the weather) – or perhaps by the weather (with a little help from Drake) – and a fledging overseas empire began to take shape.

*This part may well not be true. Especially the Tudor car park bit.

Now is the Winter of our Disco Tent

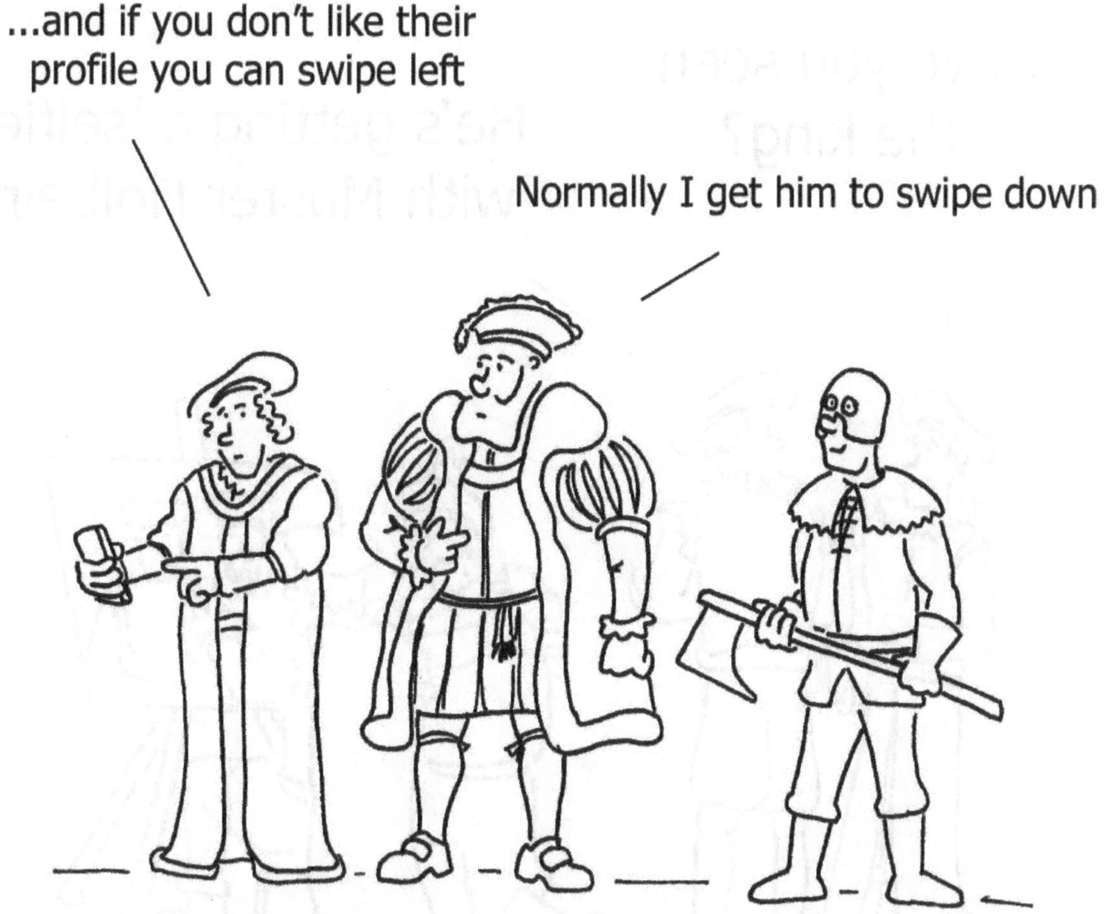
...and if you don't like their profile you can swipe left
Normally I get him to swipe down

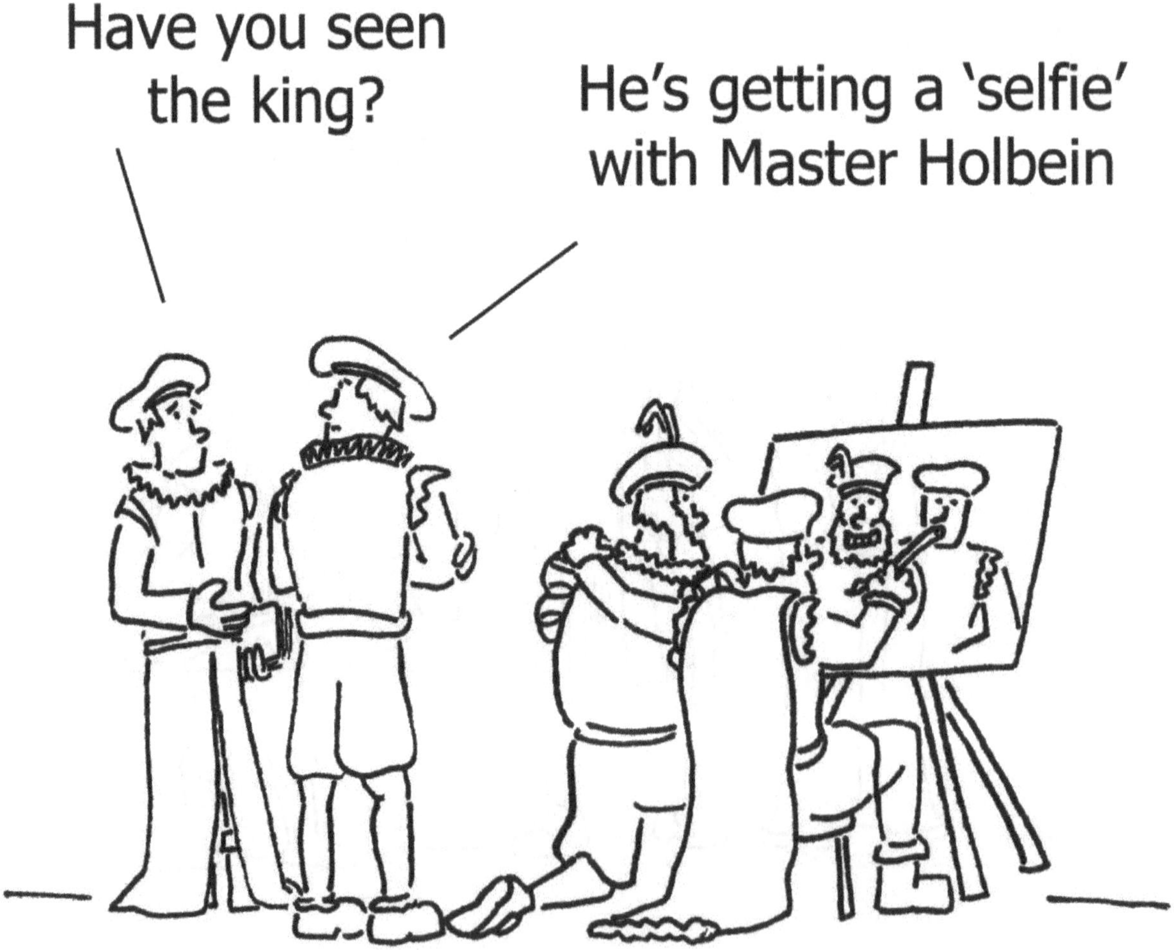
Have you seen the king?
He's getting a 'selfie' with Master Holbein

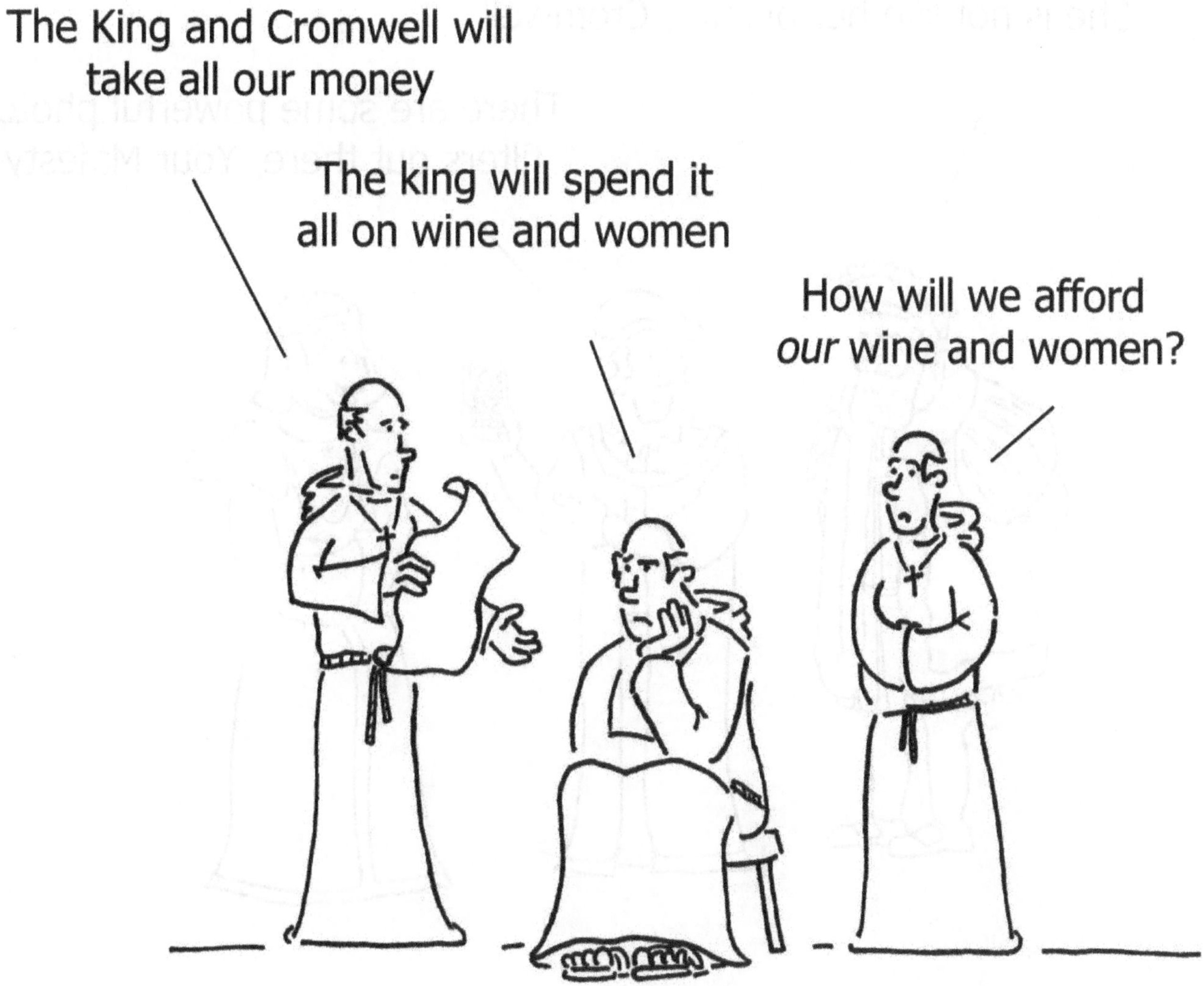

The King and Cromwell will take all our money
The king will spend it all on wine and women
How will we afford *our* wine and women?

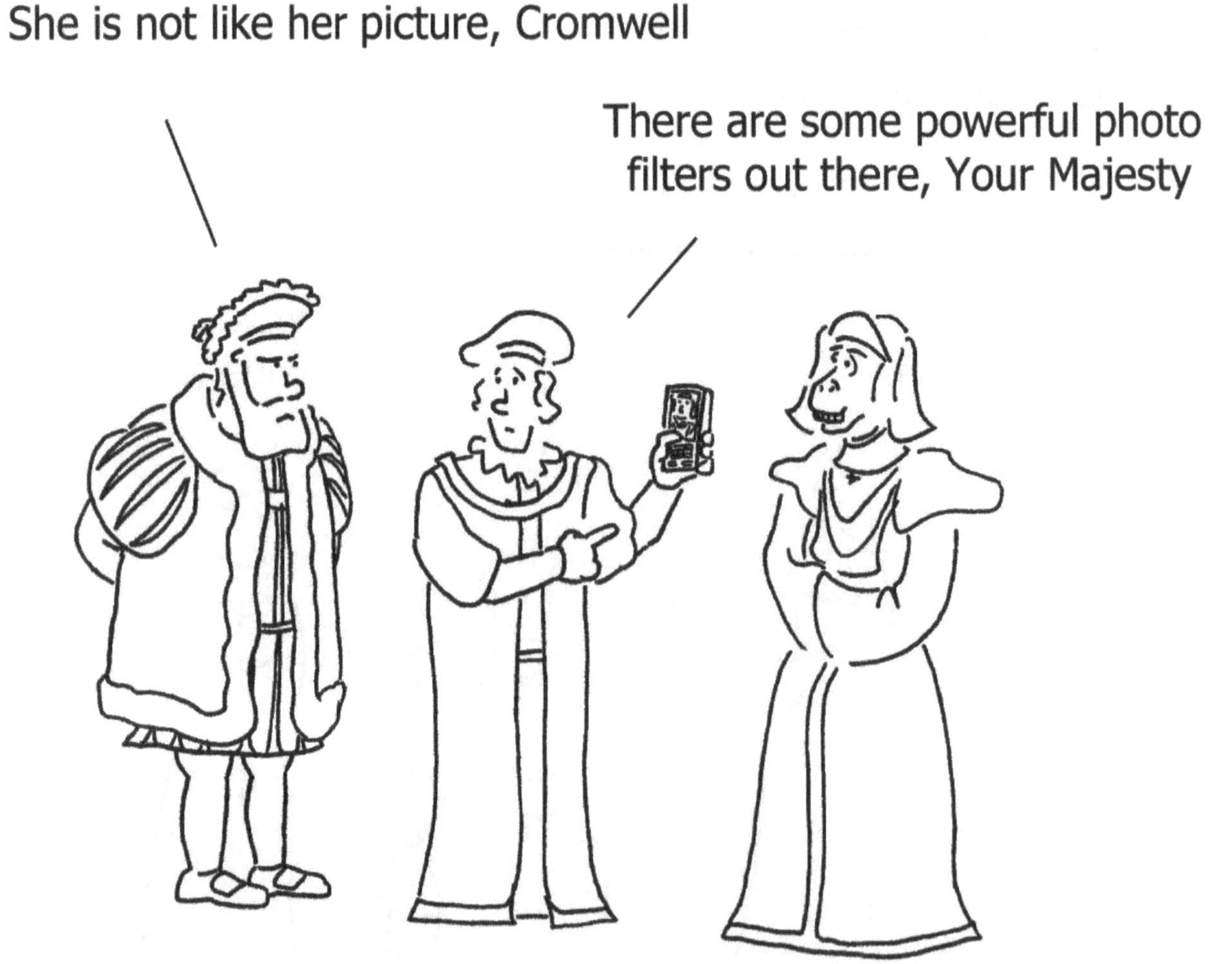
She is not like her picture, Cromwell
There are some powerful photo filters out there, Your Majesty

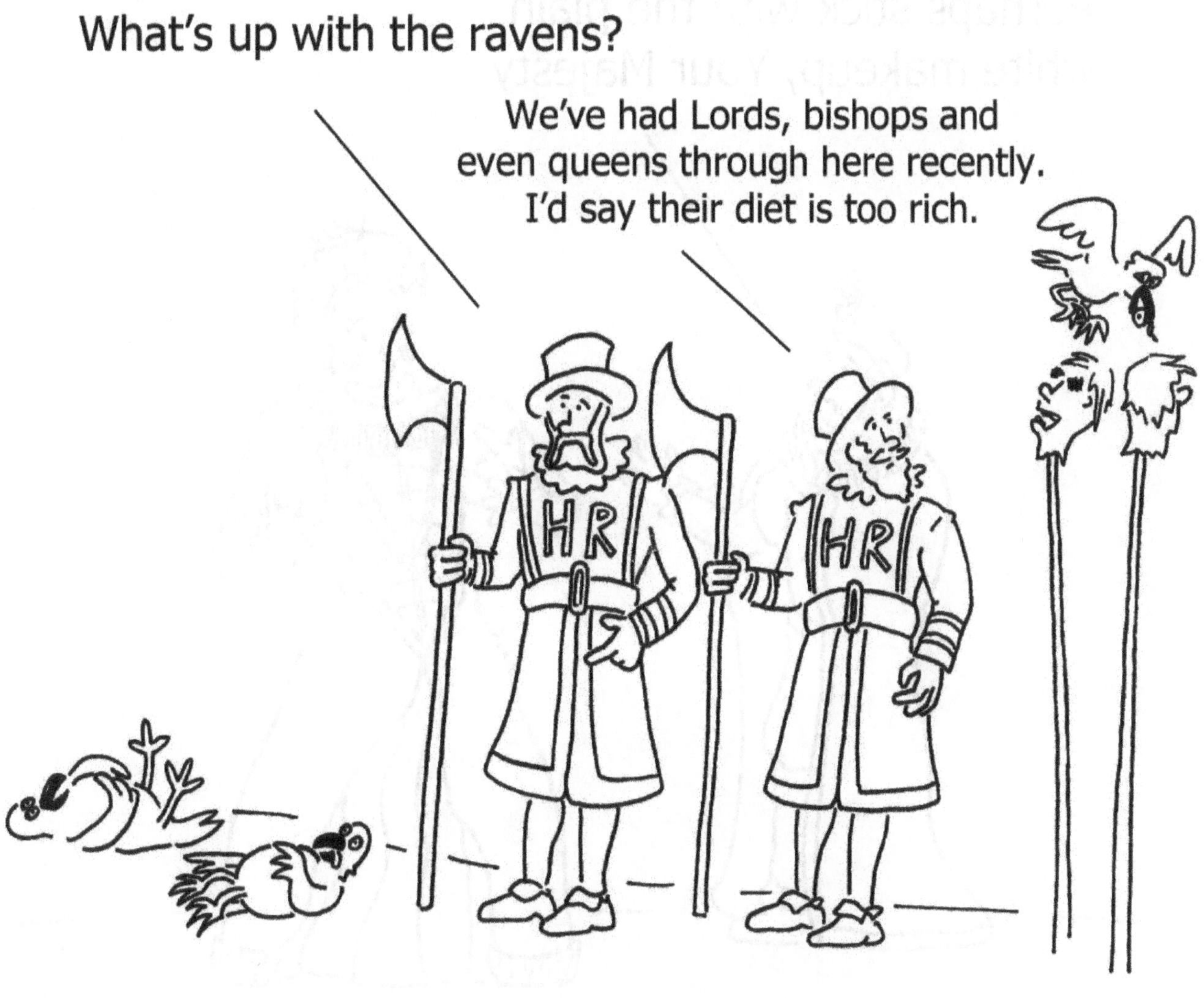
What's up with the ravens?
We've had Lords, bishops and even queens through here recently. I'd say their diet is too rich.
HR
HR

The Tower of London

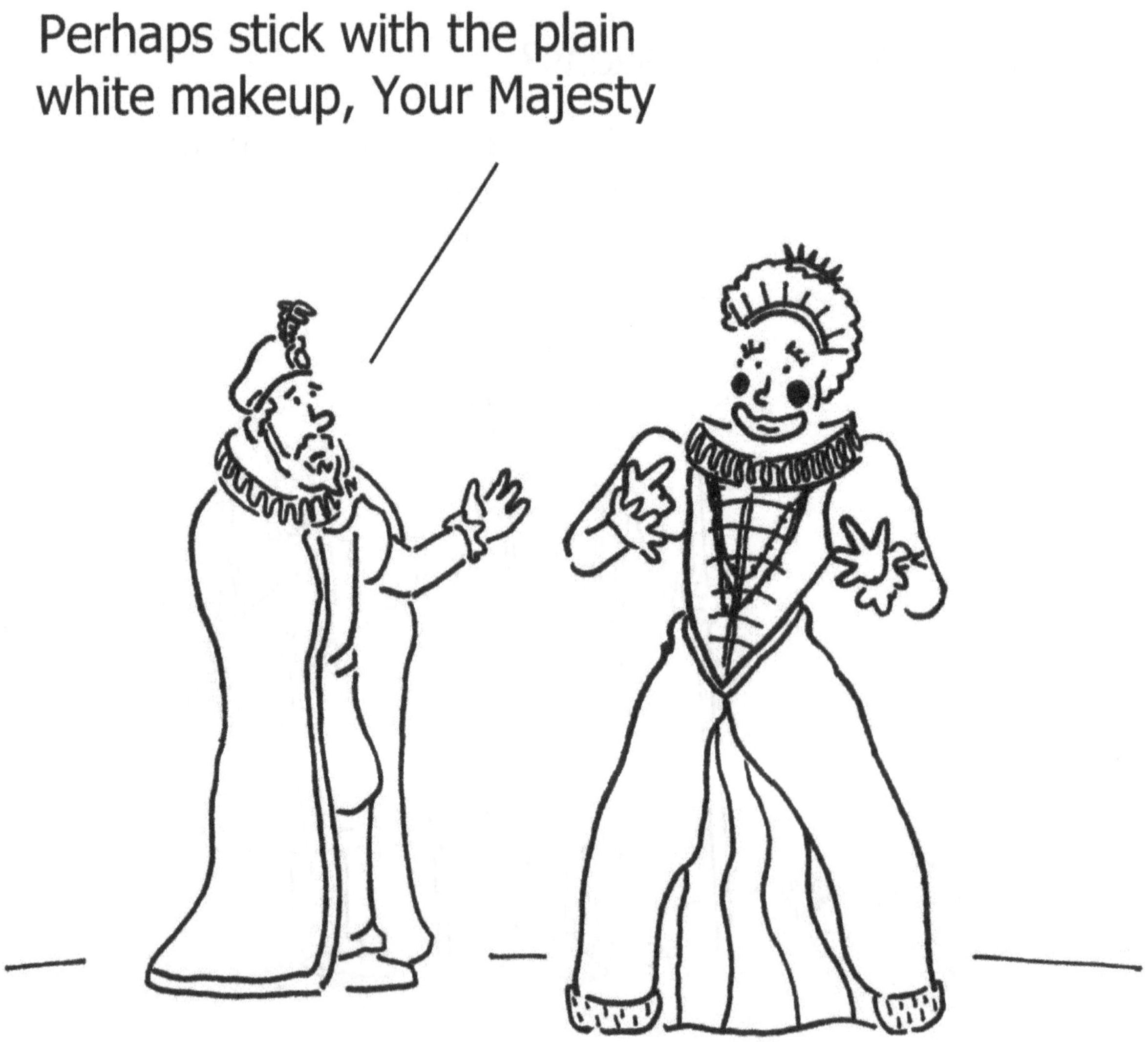
Perhaps stick with the plain white makeup, Your Majesty

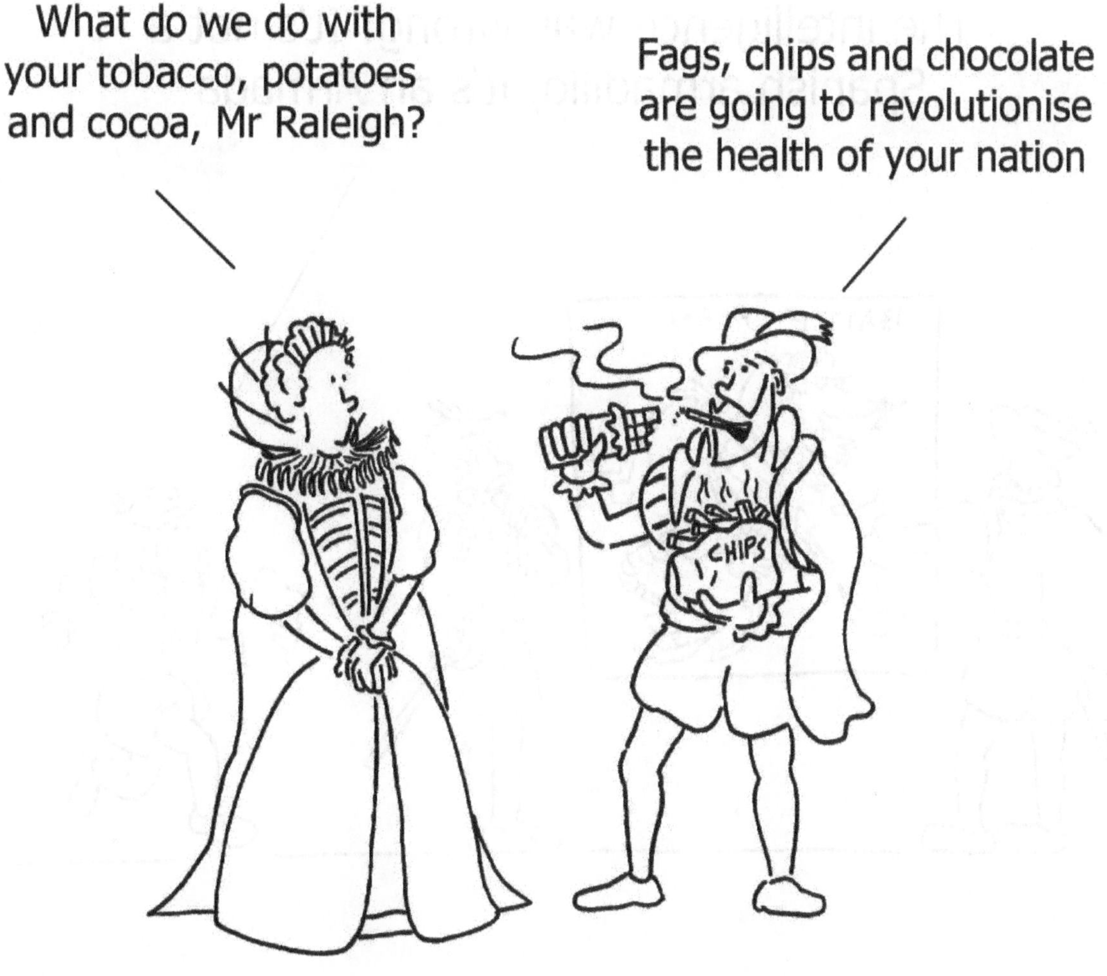
What do we do with your tobacco, potatoes and cocoa, Mr Raleigh?
Fags, chips and chocolate are going to revolutionise the health of your nation
CHIPS

The intelligence was wrong! It’s not a Spanish armadillo, it’s an Armada

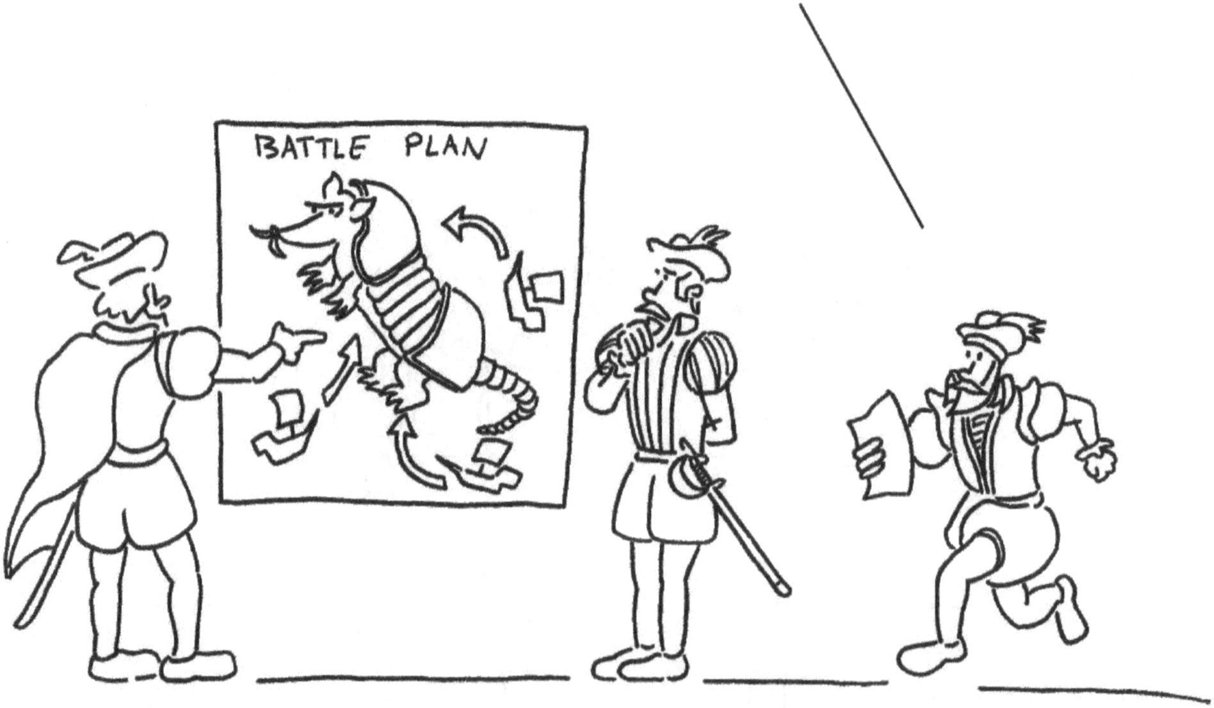
BATTLE PLAN

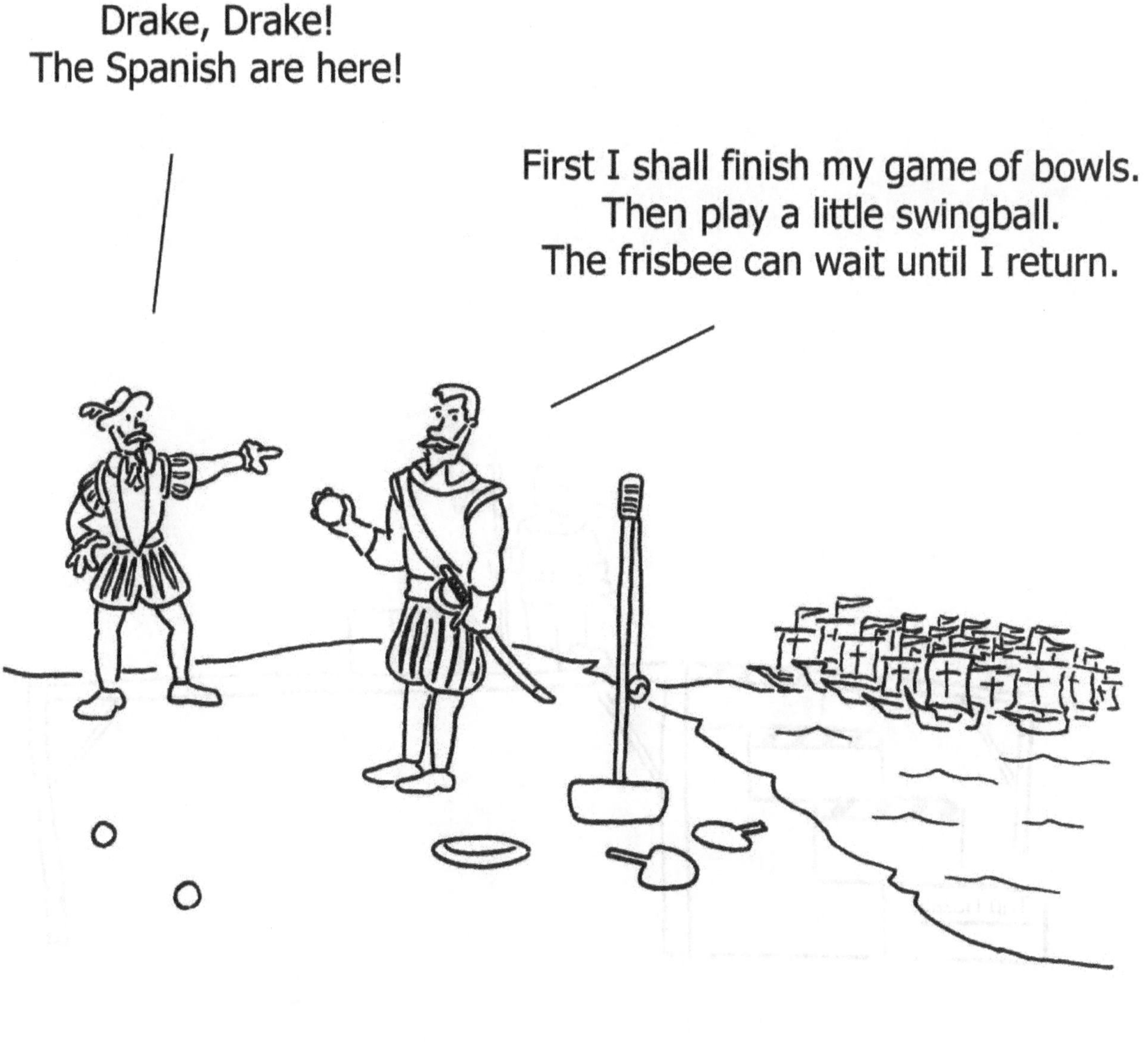
Drake, Drake!
The Spanish are here!
First I shall finish my game of bowls.
Then play a little swingball.
The frisbee can wait until I return.

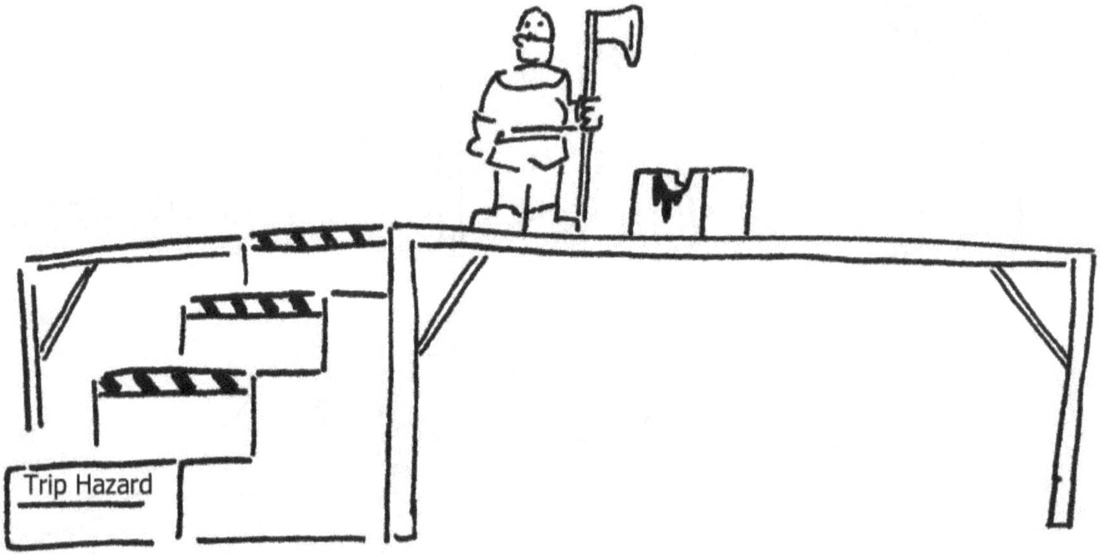
Trip Hazard

The Stuarts

Often the first thing to strike people about the Stuart dynasty is the Stuartless bit in the middle. The interregnum rule by Cromwells senior and junior was the country's only time spent as a republic. It came about as a result of a civil war which was (like most wars?) a huge mess.

So much of a mess, in fact, that it was really a series of wars in which all four corners of Britain repeatedly came together to knock lumps out of each other and themselves. The end result* was the execution of Charles I and a brief experiment in life without a monarchy that was never going to last once Cromwell banned Christmas and football.

Prior to the wars, James I had ruled over a nation in the grip of witch hunting fever and survived an assassination attempt by a group of religious fundamentalist terrorists who (may or may not have) modelled themselves on the online activist group Anonymous. After the interregnum, Charles II's reign included forays by the Dutch up the Thames, a resurgence of the plague and the Great Fire of London. Charles was quite pre-occupied with his own gratification but probably noticed these events.

*It has been argued that both sides carried on the fighting across the Atlantic in what became the American Revolutionary War and that the end result was actually the birth of the United States of America.

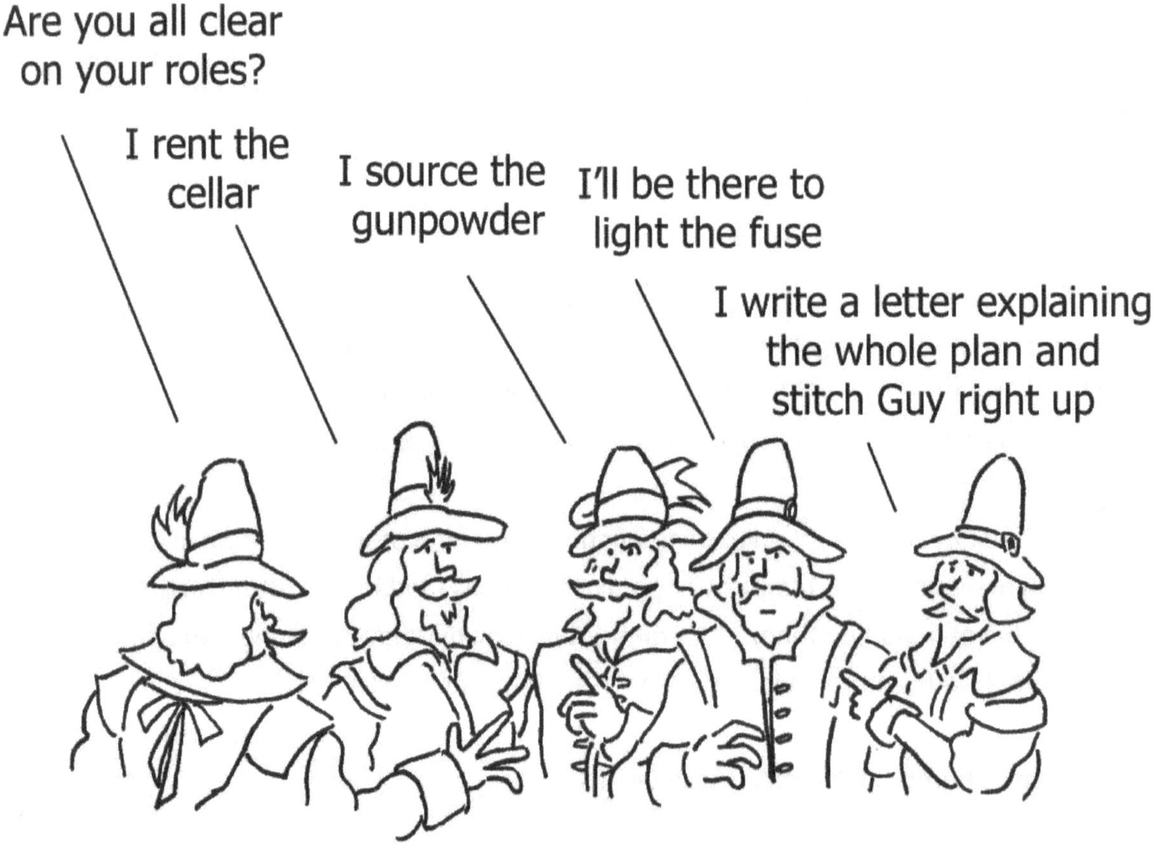
Are you all clear on your roles?
I rent the cellar
I source the gunpowder
I'll be there to light the fuse
I write a letter explaining the whole plan and stitch Guy right up

The Gunpowder Plot

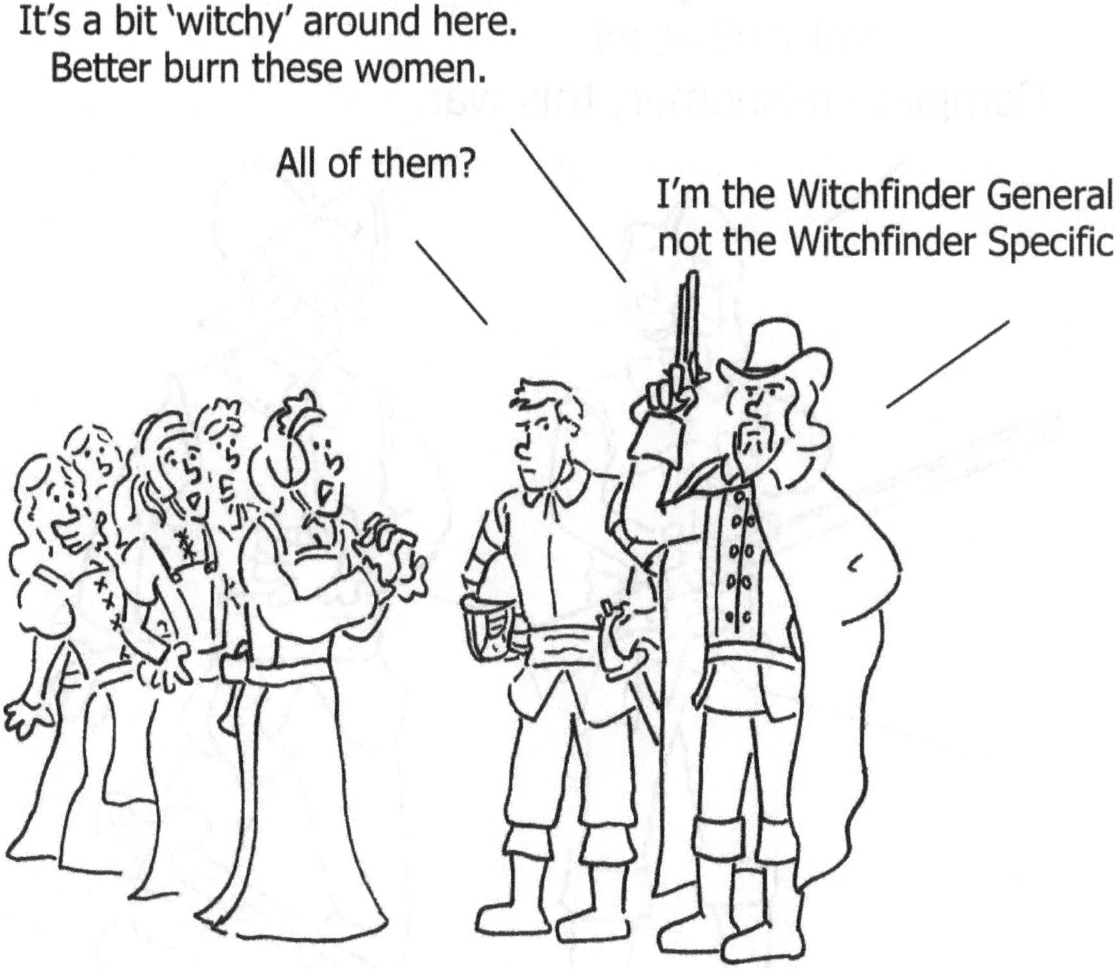
It’s a bit ‘witchy’ around here.
Better burn these women.
All of them?
I’m the Witchfinder General
not the Witchfinder Specific

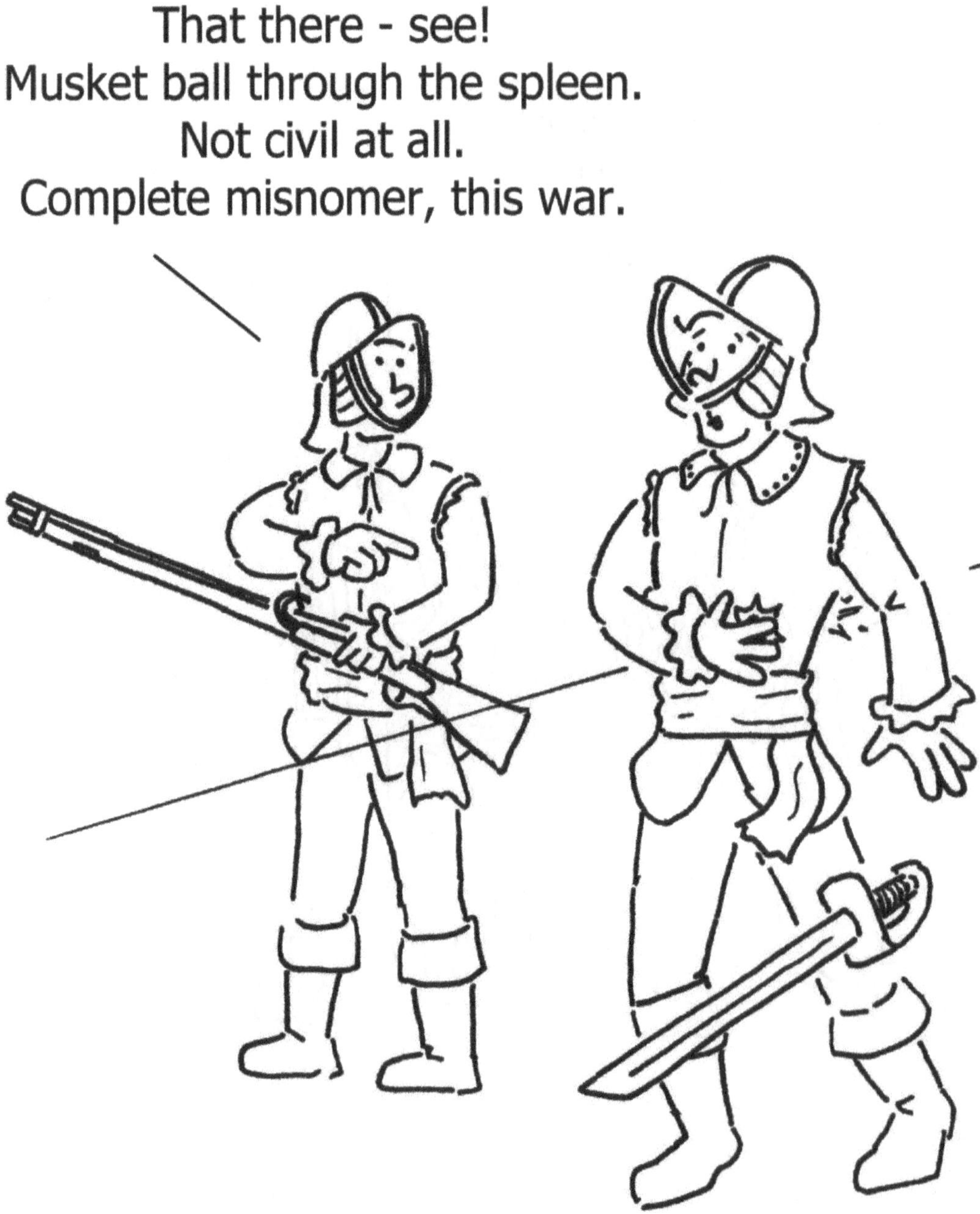
That there - see!
Musket ball through the spleen.
Not civil at all.
Complete misnomer, this war.

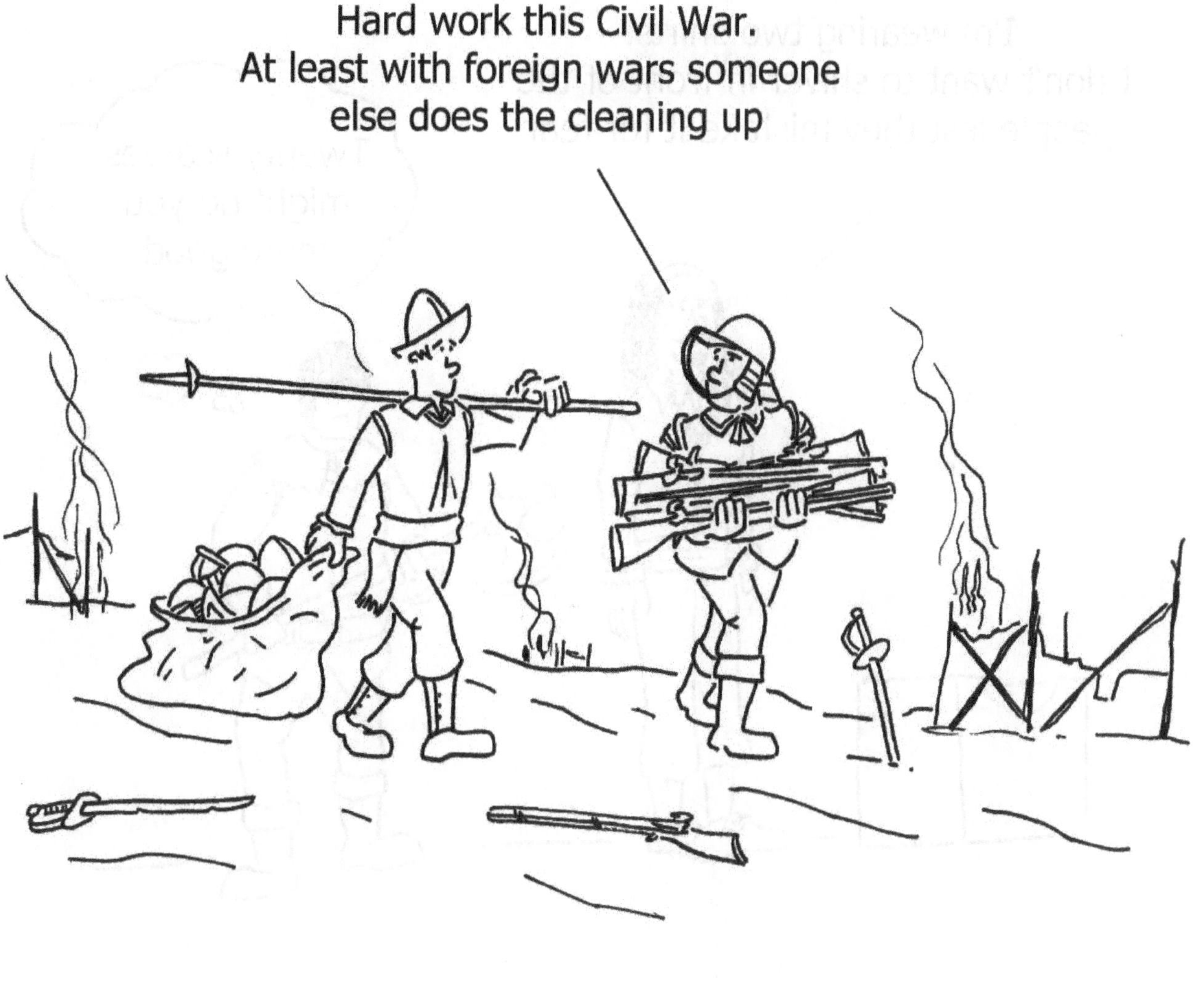
Hard work this Civil War.
At least with foreign wars someone
else does the cleaning up

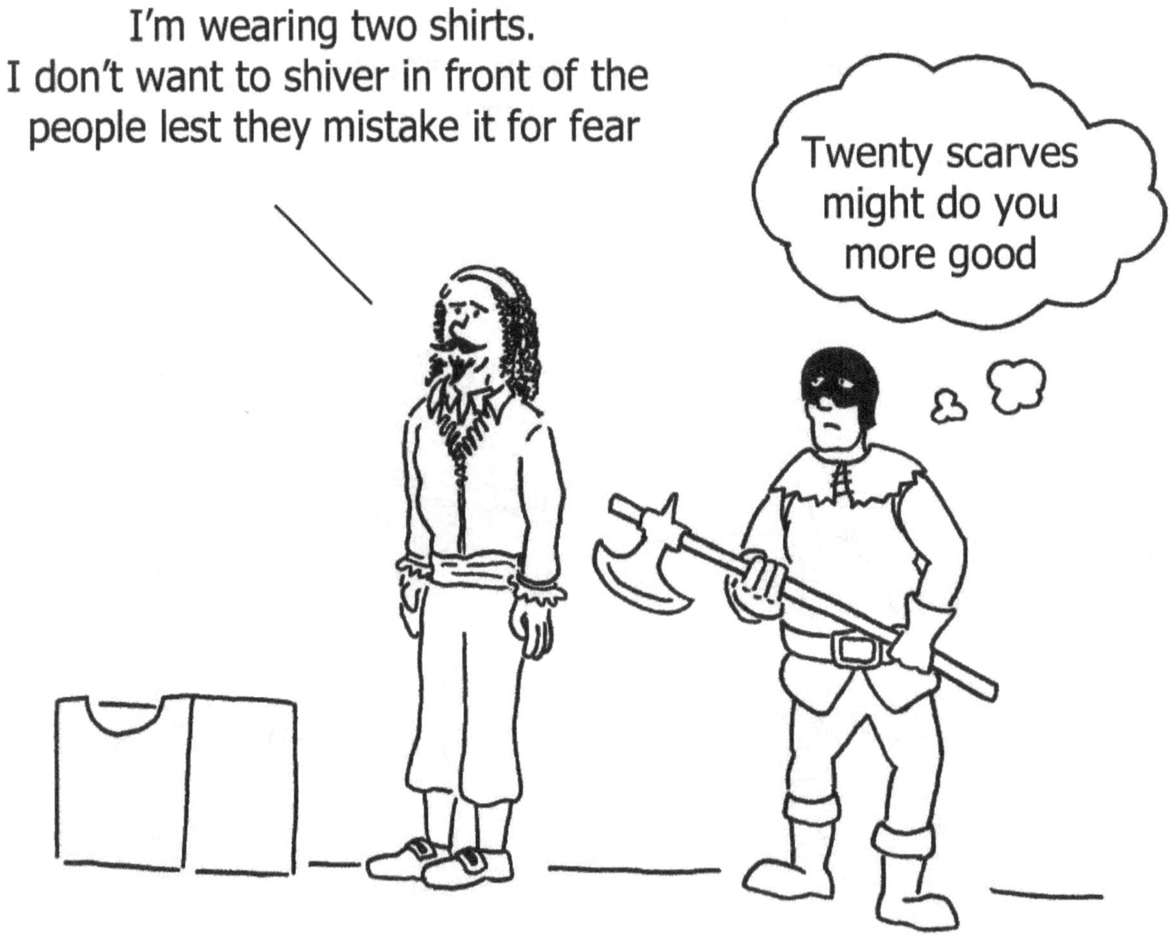
I'm wearing two shirts.
I don't want to shiver in front of the people lest they mistake it for fear
Twenty scarves might do you more good

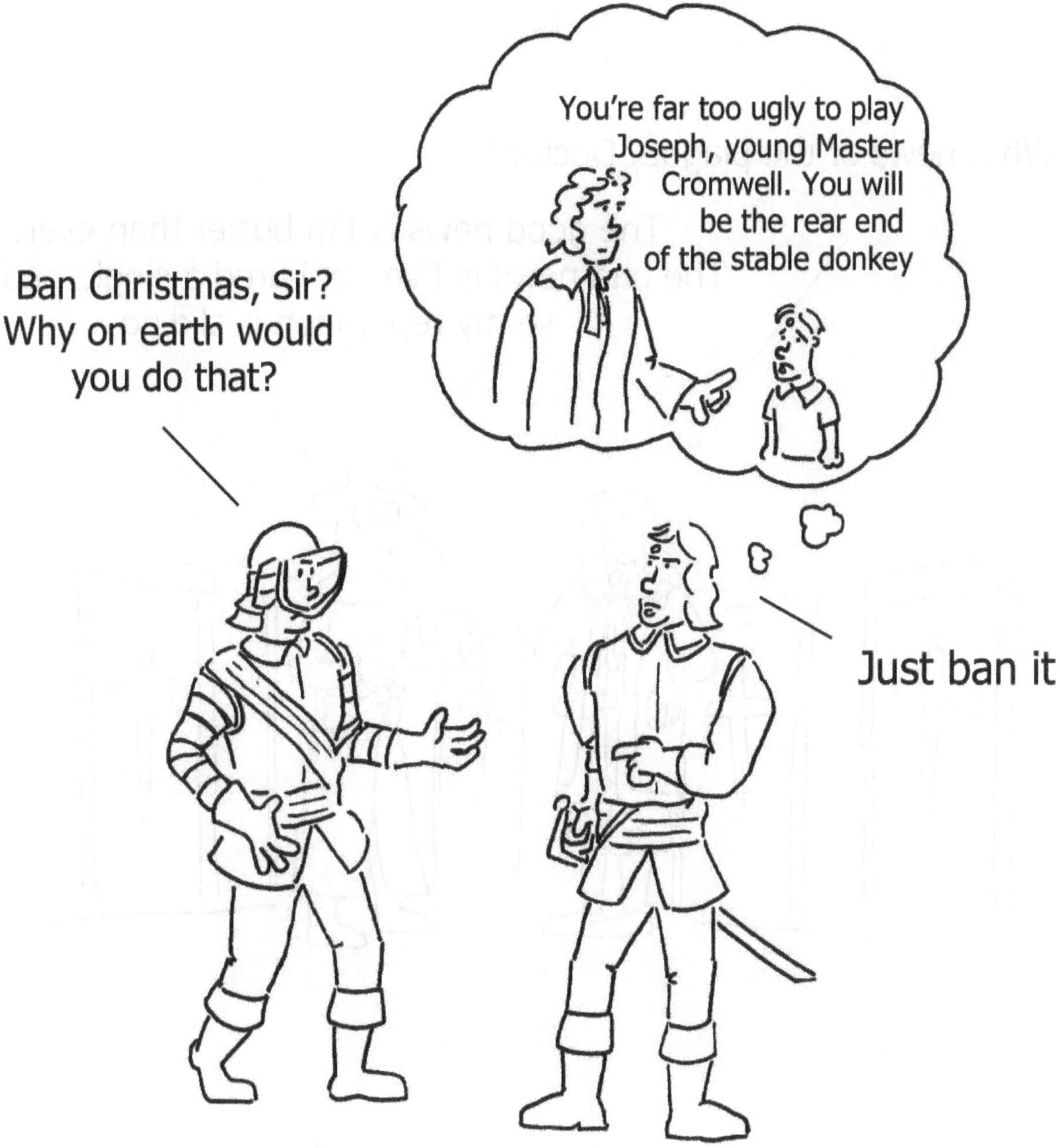

Ban Christmas, Sir? Why on earth would you do that?
You're far too ugly to play Joseph, young Master Cromwell. You will be the rear end of the stable donkey
Just ban it

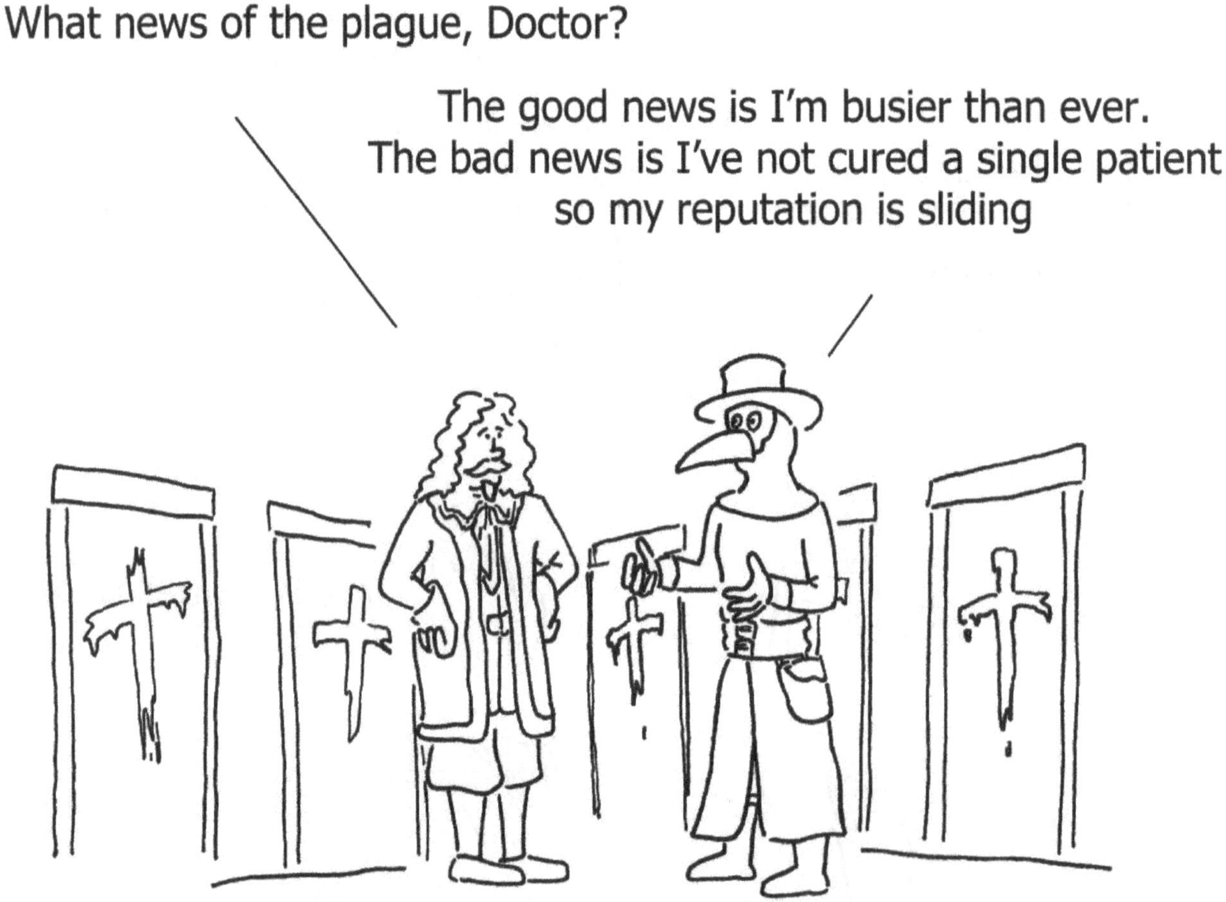
What news of the plague, Doctor?
The good news is I'm busier than ever. The bad news is I've not cured a single patient so my reputation is sliding

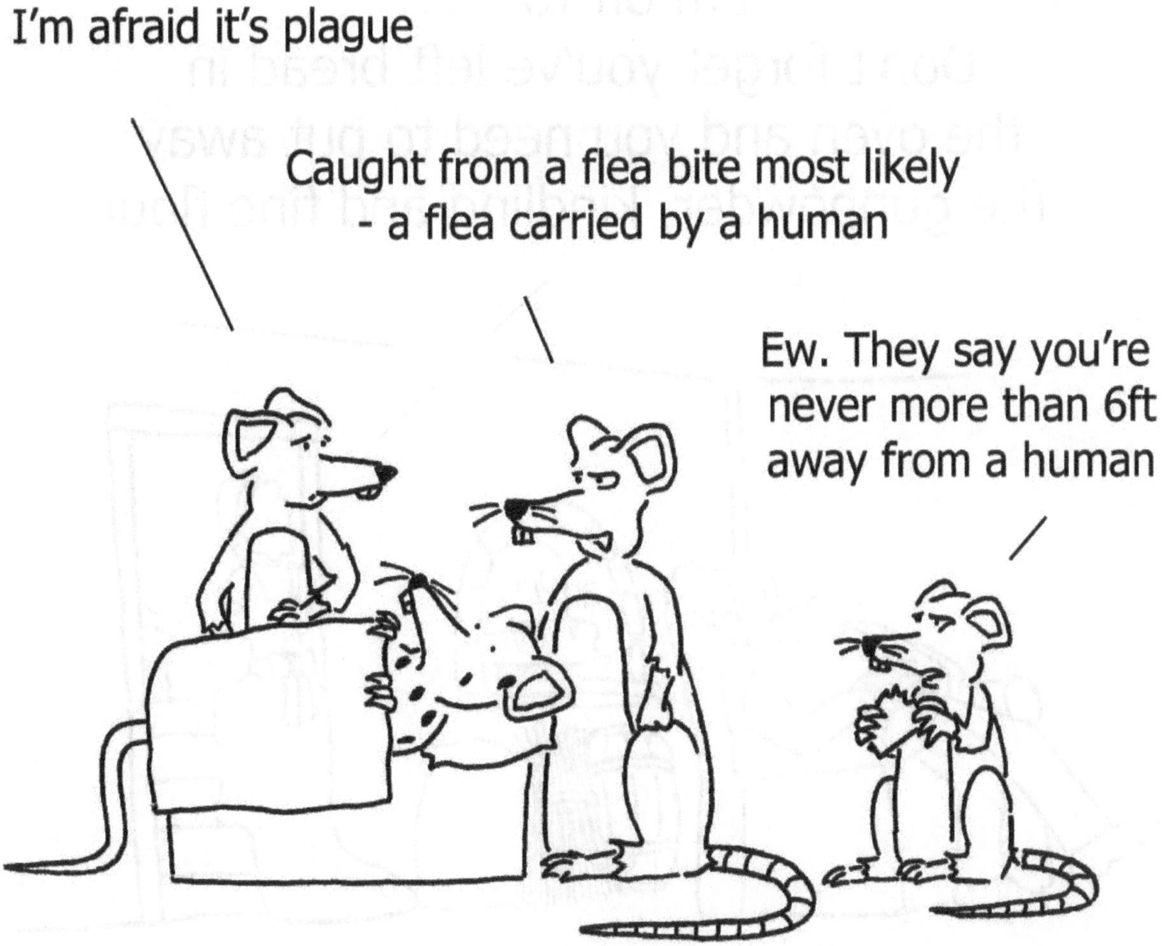
I'm afraid it's plague
Caught from a flea bite most likely - a flea carried by a human
Ew. They say you're never more than 6ft away from a human

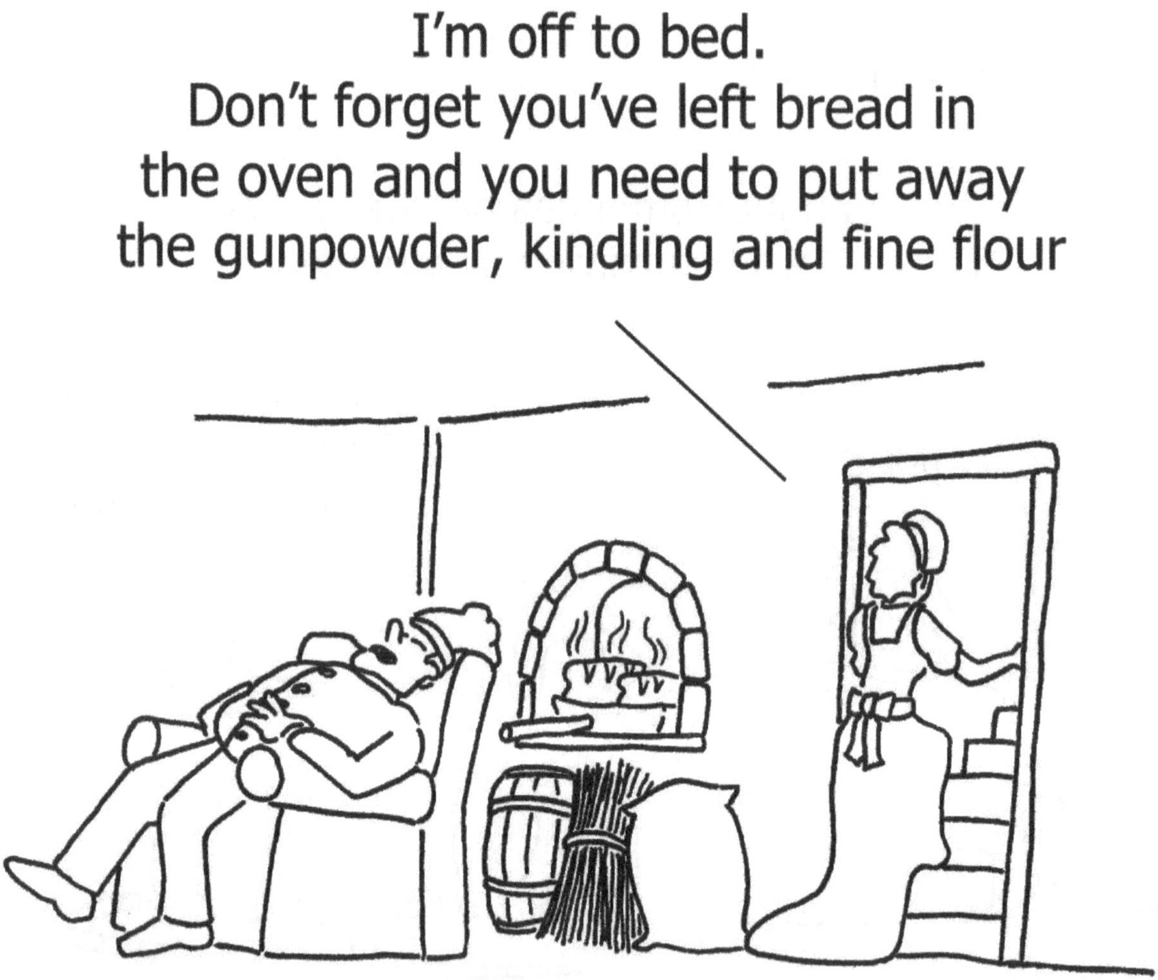
I'm off to bed.
Don't forget you've left bread in the oven and you need to put away the gunpowder, kindling and fine flour

Pudding Lane 1666

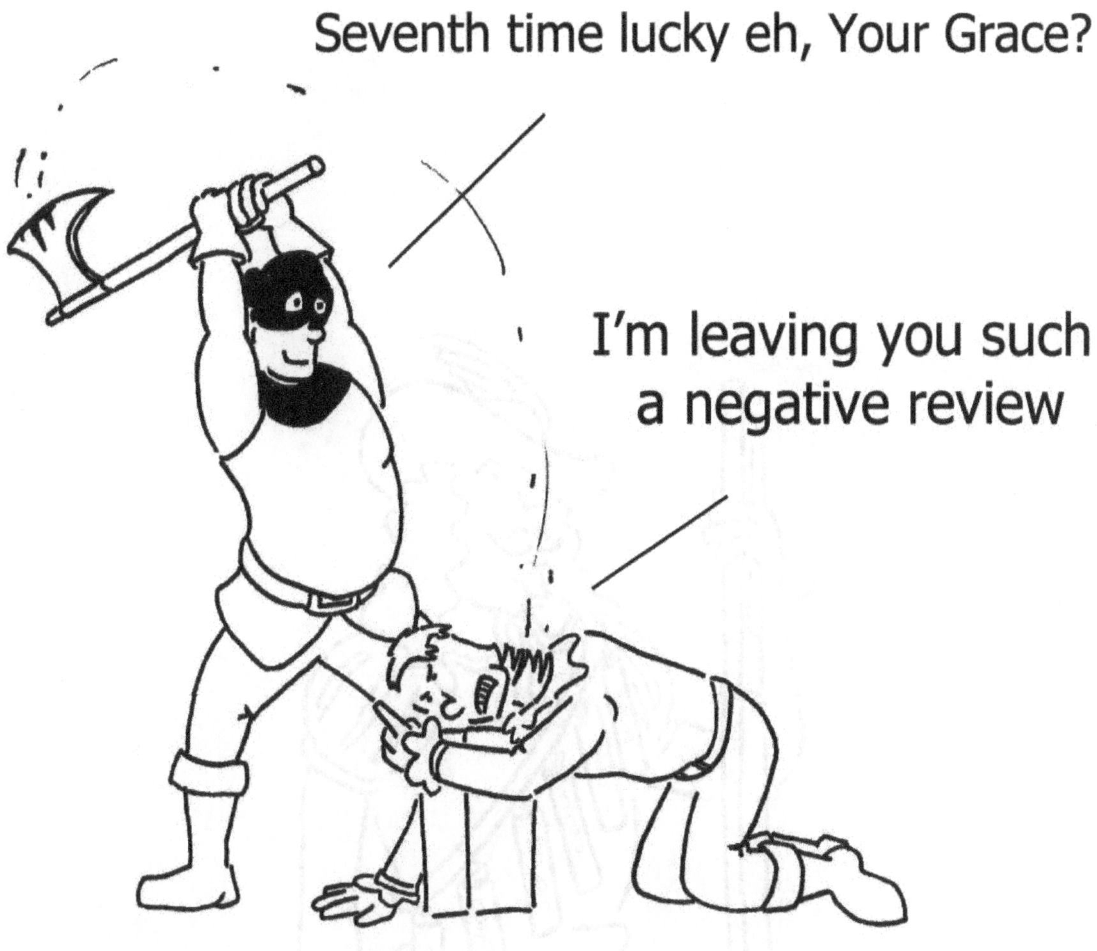

The Monmouth Rebellion ends... eventually

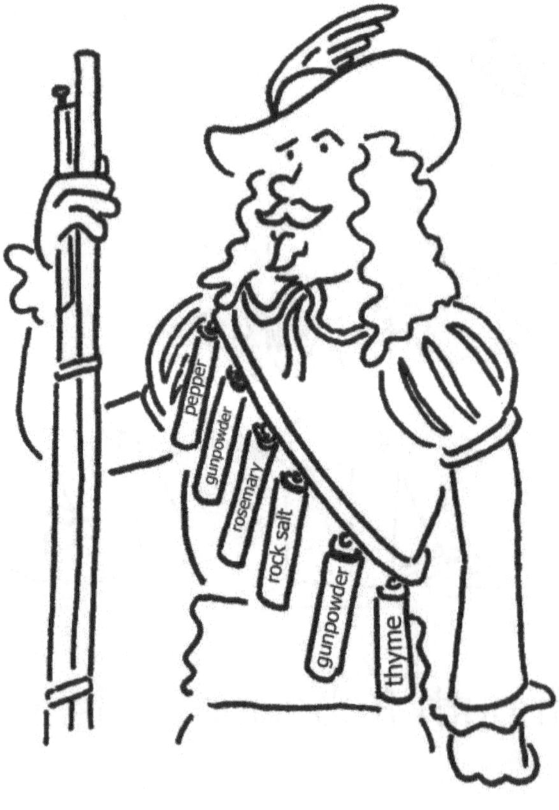
pepper
gunpowder
rosemary
rock salt
gunpowder
thyme

The Georgians

Though named after the four Hanoverian Georges who wore the crown, the Georgian period also includes William IV. The Stuarts were not completely out of the picture either, their final rising (and falling) taking place at Culloden.

Culloden is interesting not just because it was the last battle fought on British soil but because, despite its reputation as a 'Calcutta Cup' England vs Scotland affair, more Scots fought on the Hanoverian side than the Stuart.

The Georgian era was the age of the outlaw. Pirates roamed the Caribbean, smugglers dodged the Riding Officers and highwaymen threatened travellers on the road. Punishments for these ne'er-do-wells included hanging, branding, whipping or transportation to Australia. From this selection, only the last has become a popular gap year option.

Criminals could avoid transportation if they agreed to join the military – which was very busy indeed during this time. Trafalgar and Waterloo saw the end of the Napoleonic threat on sea and land respectively but when the heroes of these battles returned home, they encountered a changing landscape.

The industrial revolution was underway, mills and factories were rising up, people were moving to cities and – most unusually – the world was starting to operate according to little numbers on a clock instead of the sun rising and setting. Strange times indeed.

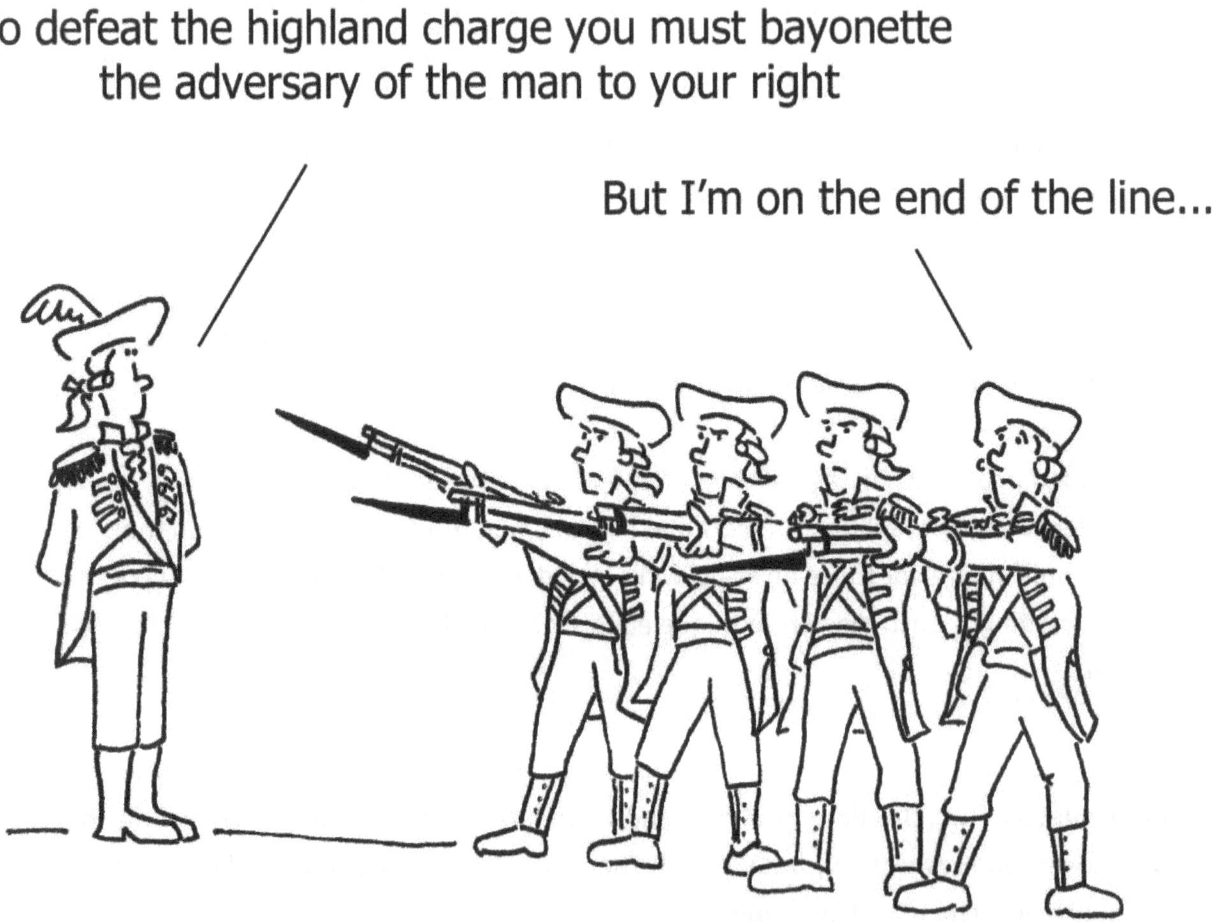
To defeat the highland charge you must bayonette the adversary of the man to your right
But I'm on the end of the line...

Training for Culloden

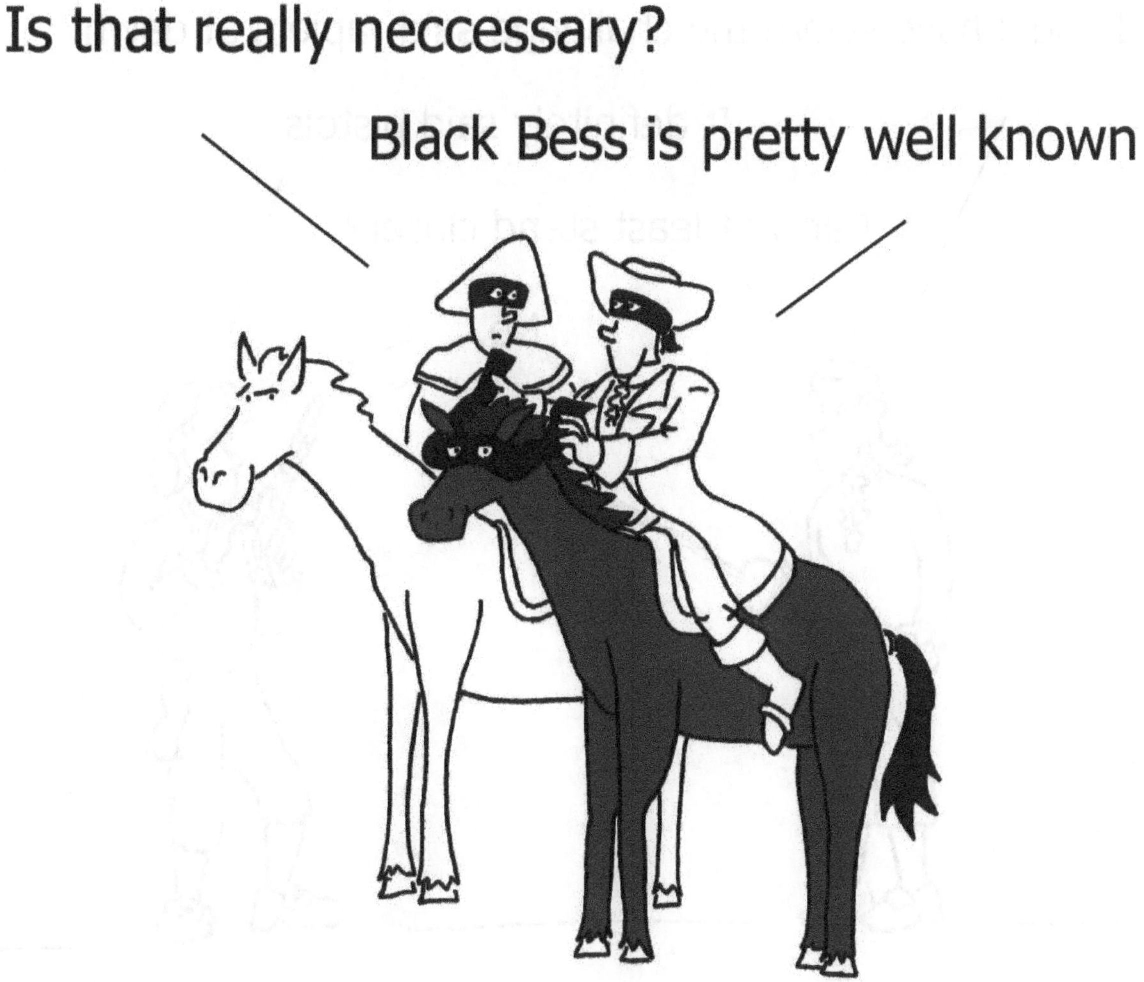
Is that really neccessary?
Black Bess is pretty well known

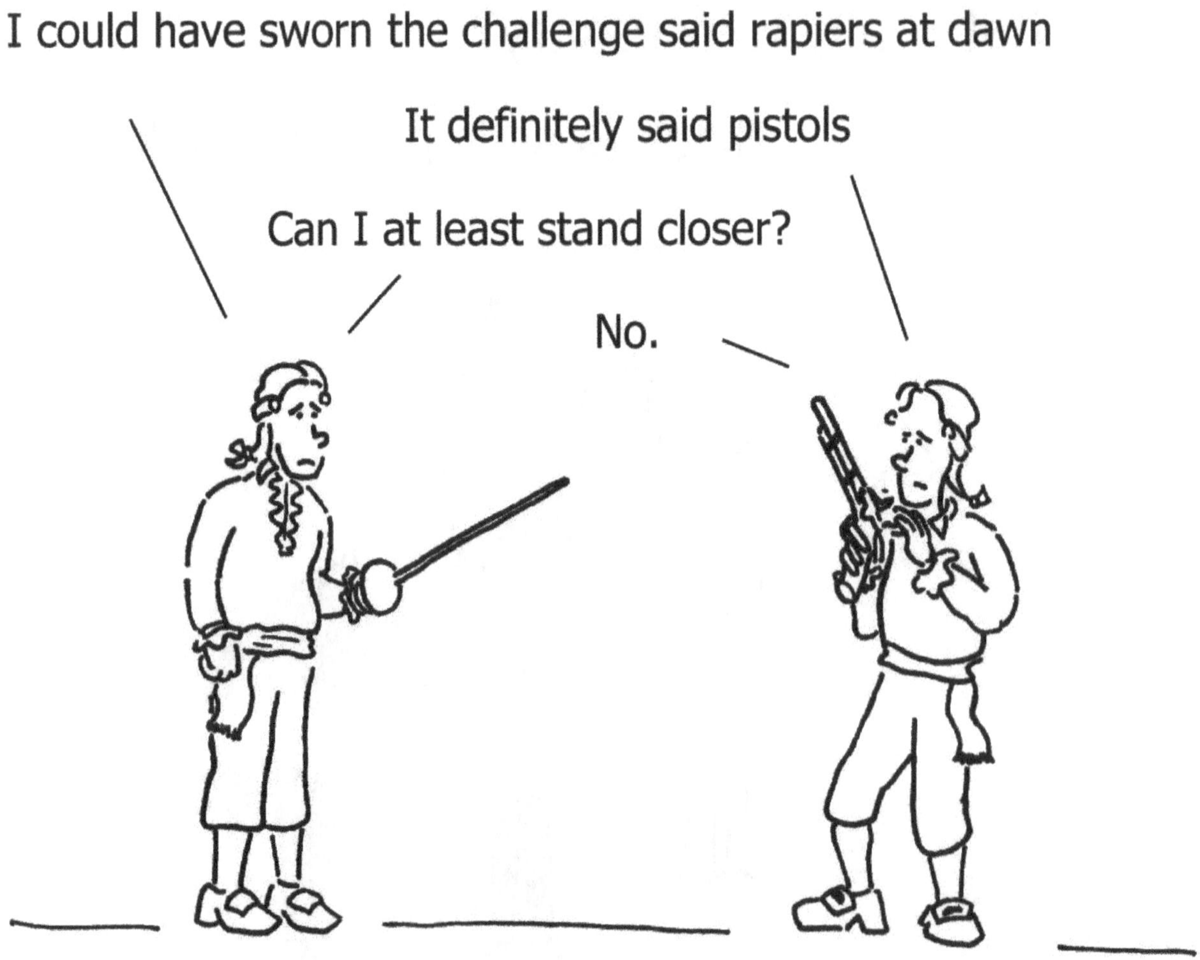
I could have sworn the challenge said rapiers at dawn
It definitely said pistols
Can I at least stand closer?
No.

I warned you not to make the buffet too appetising

Explosive Corset Failure

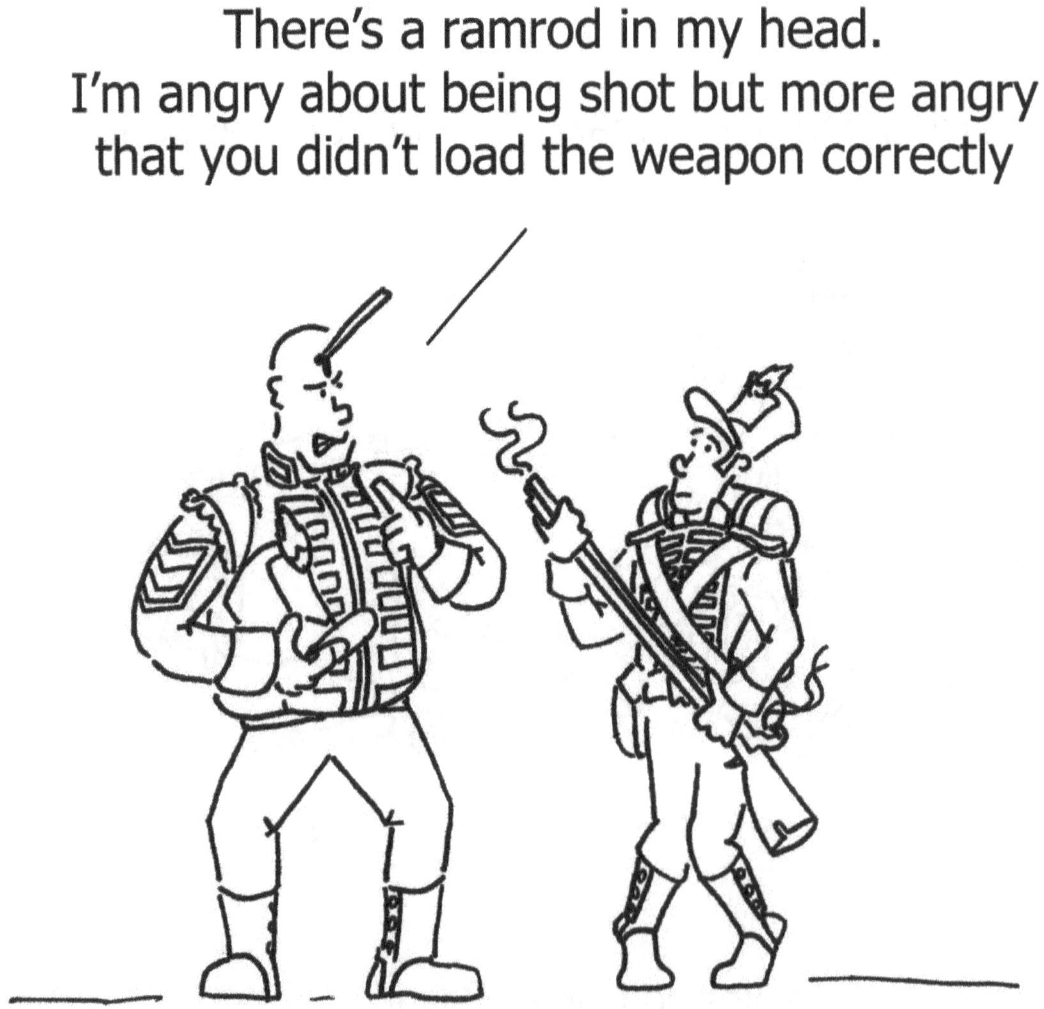
There's a ramrod in my head.
I'm angry about being shot but more angry
that you didn't load the weapon correctly

Musket Drill

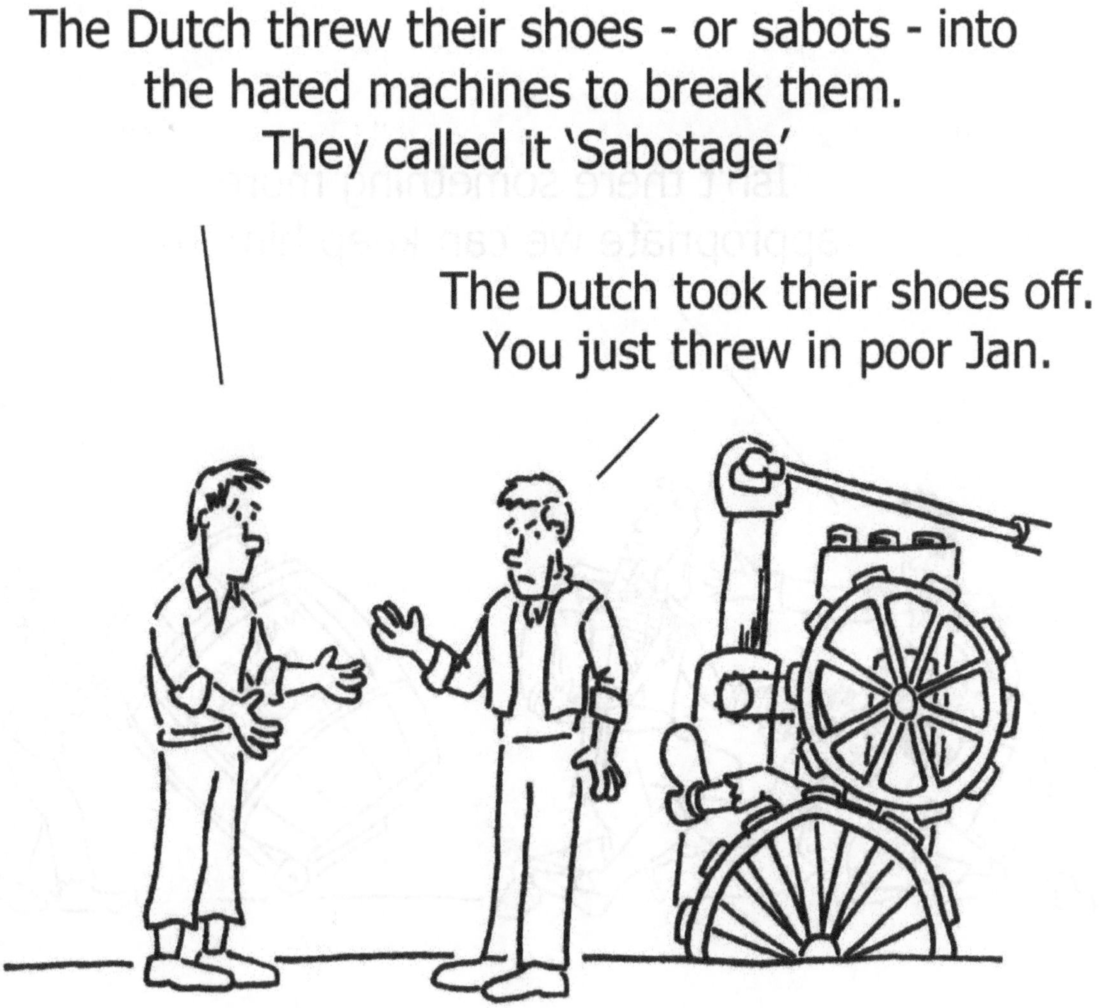
The Dutch threw their shoes - or sabots - into the hated machines to break them. They called it 'Sabotage'
The Dutch took their shoes off. You just threw in poor Jan.

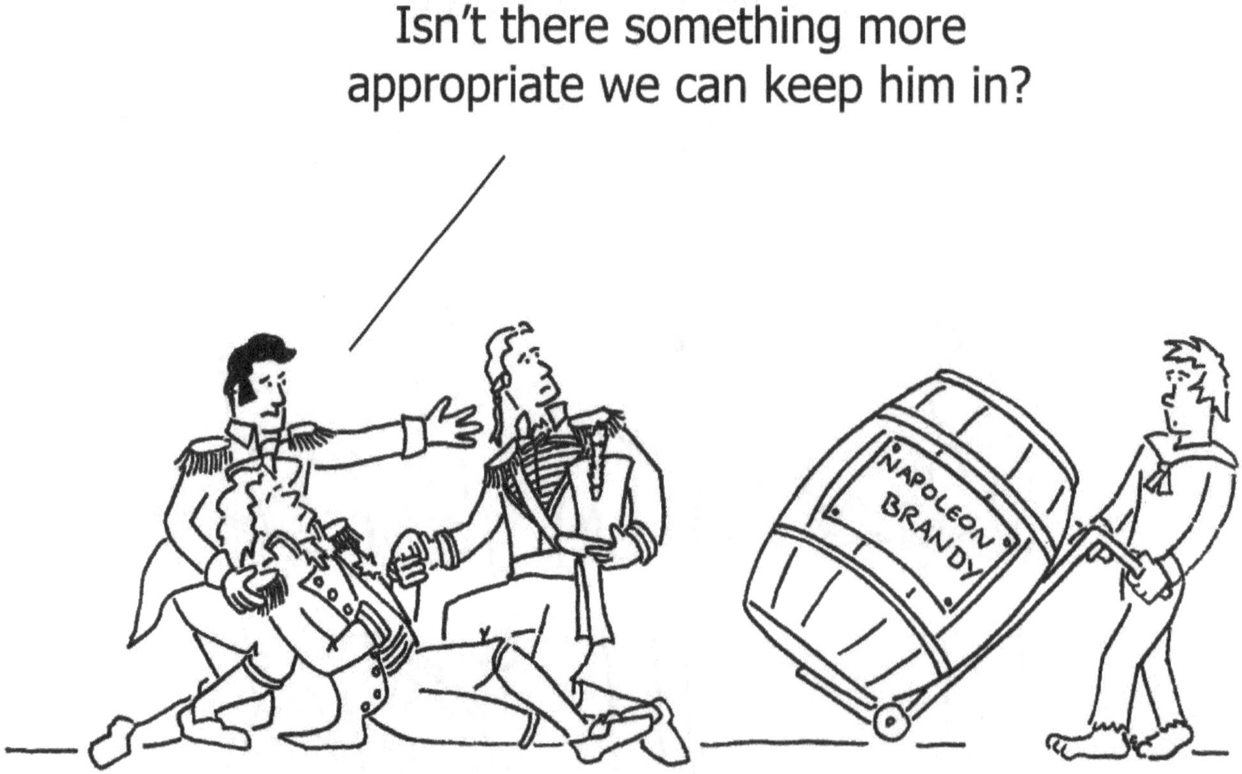
Isn't there something more appropriate we can keep him in?
NAPOLEON BRANDY

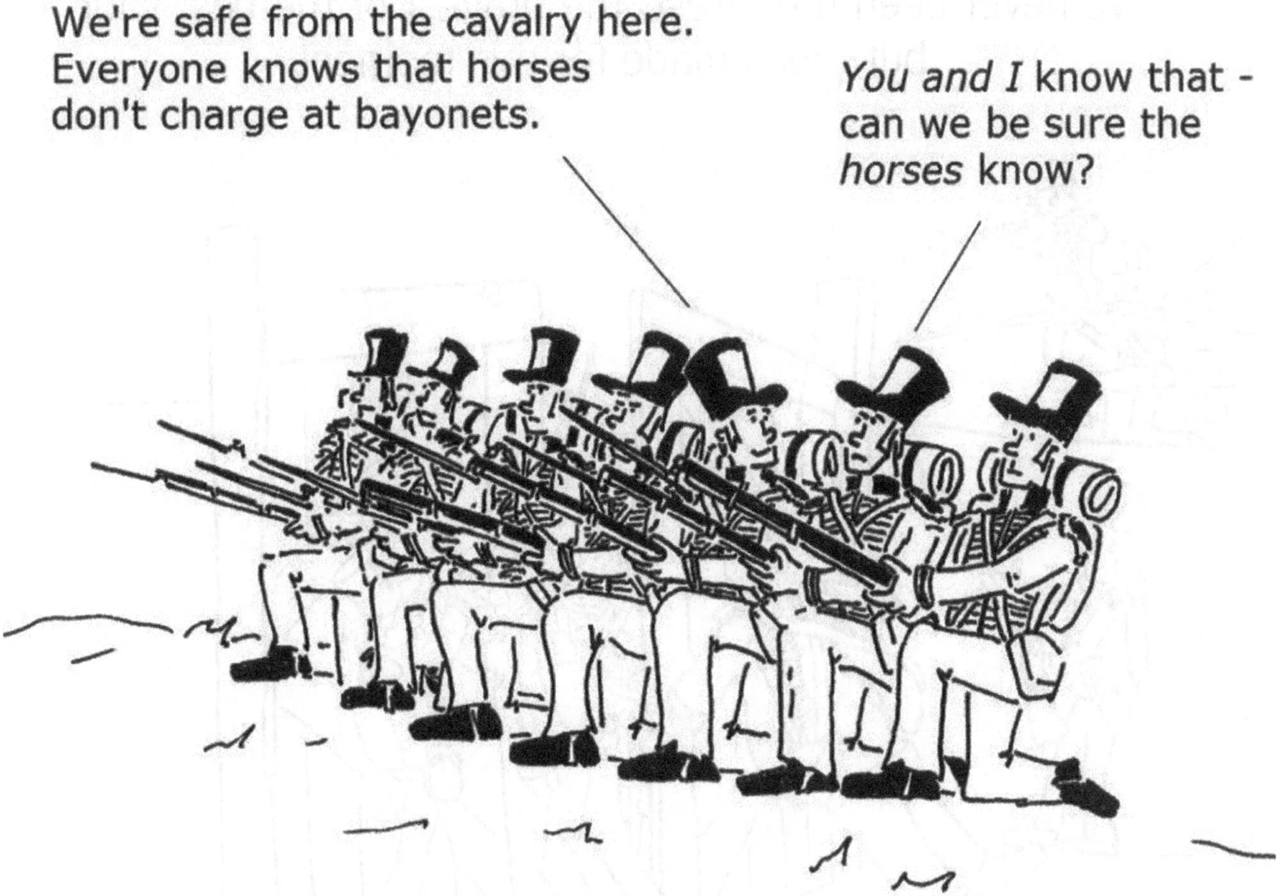
We're safe from the cavalry here. Everyone knows that horses don't charge at bayonets.
You and I know that - can we be sure the *horses* know?

Waterloo 18th June 1815

I've never been the fittest, the bravest or the best shot, but I was made for this moment

Closing the gates at Hougoumont
Waterloo 1815

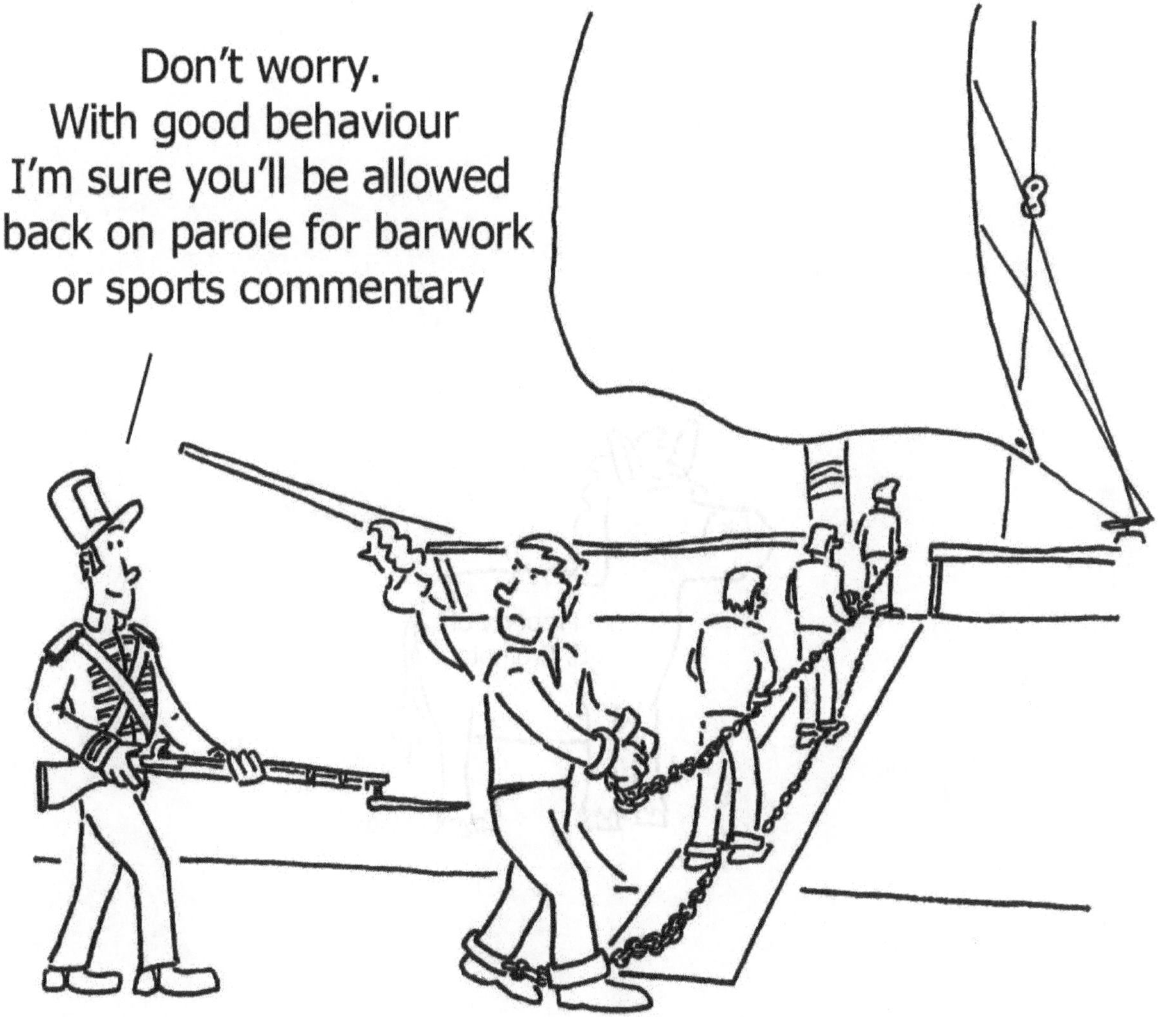
Don't worry.
With good behaviour
I'm sure you'll be allowed
back on parole for barwork
or sports commentary

Transportation to Australia

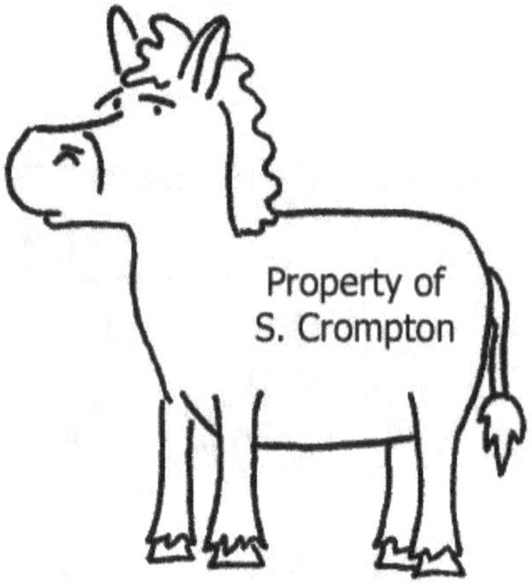
Property of
S. Crompton

The Victorians

The Victorian era is something of an anomaly in this collection as it was, on the whole, a period of peace and prosperity. Britain was the workshop of the world, the Empire was at its zenith, science and technology charged ahead, and people were terribly polite.

Happy times do not inspire as many cartoons but, never fear, there was a dark side to Victorian Britain too. Most notably in the city slums and most vividly brought to life by the works of Charles Dickens.

Yet even the darker aspects of the time were stages on a journey of progress. Throughout the nineteenth century, legislation improved working conditions, reduced child labour, introduced compulsory schooling, addressed public health, regulated housing and widened the franchise.

Yes, the big cities of the land were overpopulated, impoverished, disease-ridden open sewers but as time went on, they became less so. There was even leisure time and railways meant that sports teams could travel to play each other. This did create the need to codify the rules though – more than one football team arrived at an away match to discover their opponents played holding the ball rather than kicking it. Or vice versa.

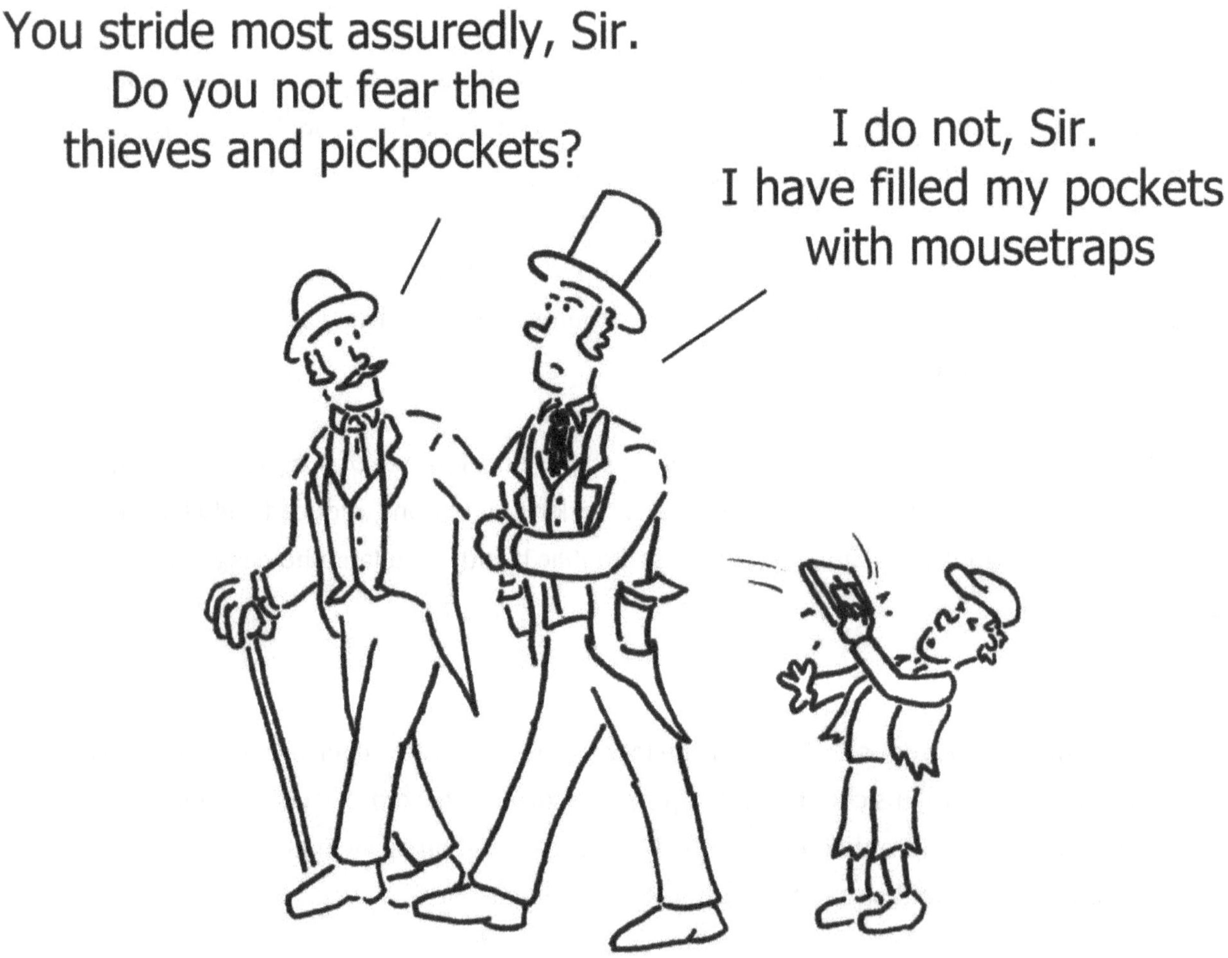
You stride most assuredly, Sir. Do you not fear the thieves and pickpockets?
I do not, Sir. I have filled my pockets with mousetraps

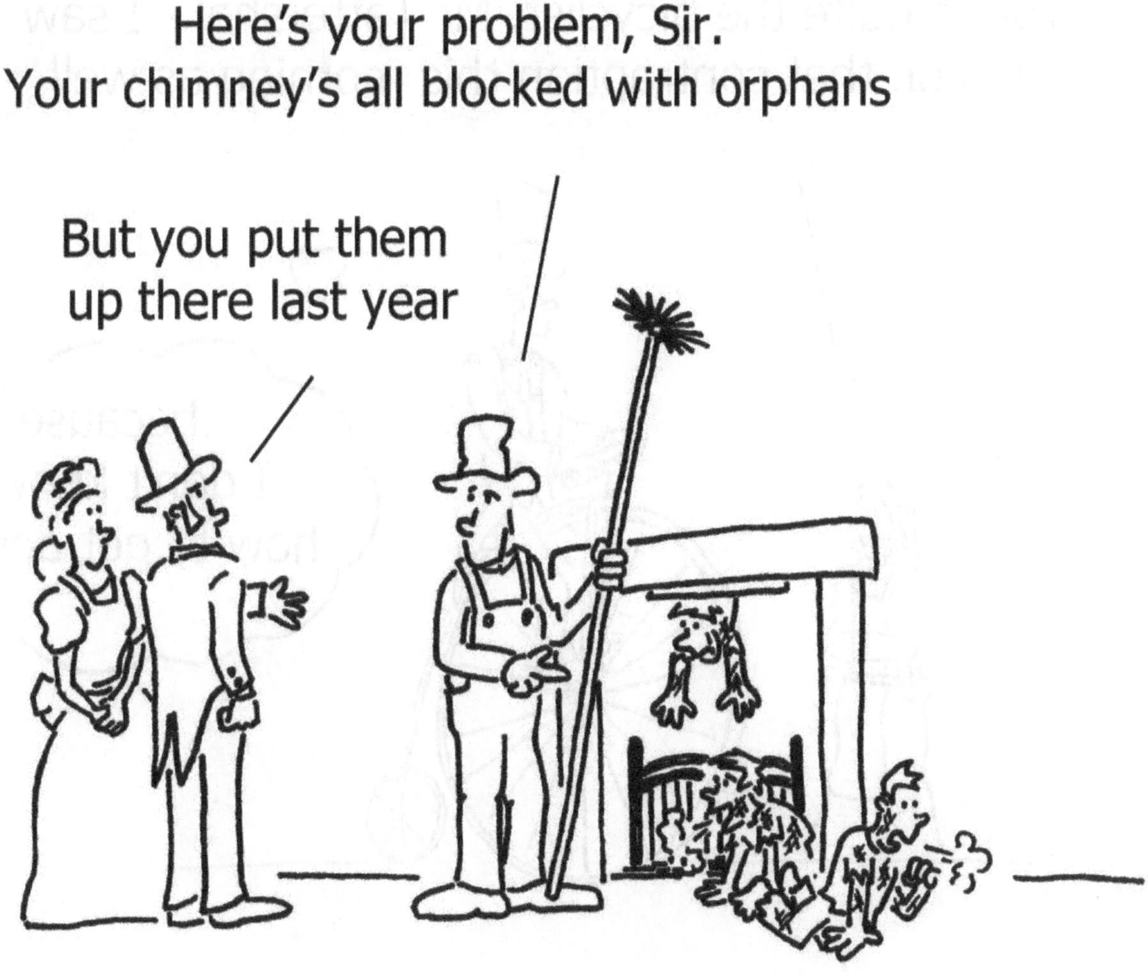
Here's your problem, Sir.
Your chimney's all blocked with orphans
But you put them
up there last year

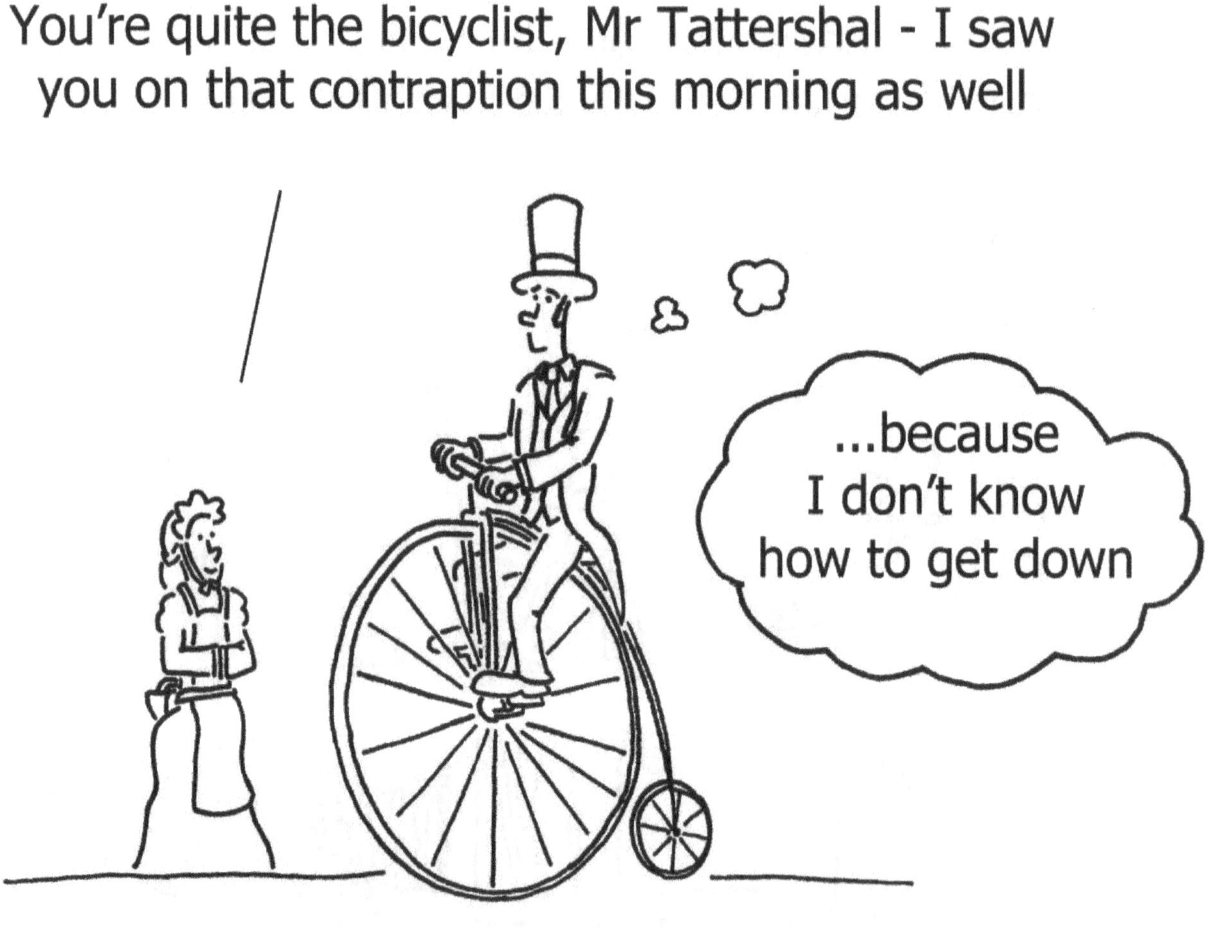
You're quite the bicyclist, Mr Tattershal - I saw you on that contraption this morning as well
...because I don't know how to get down

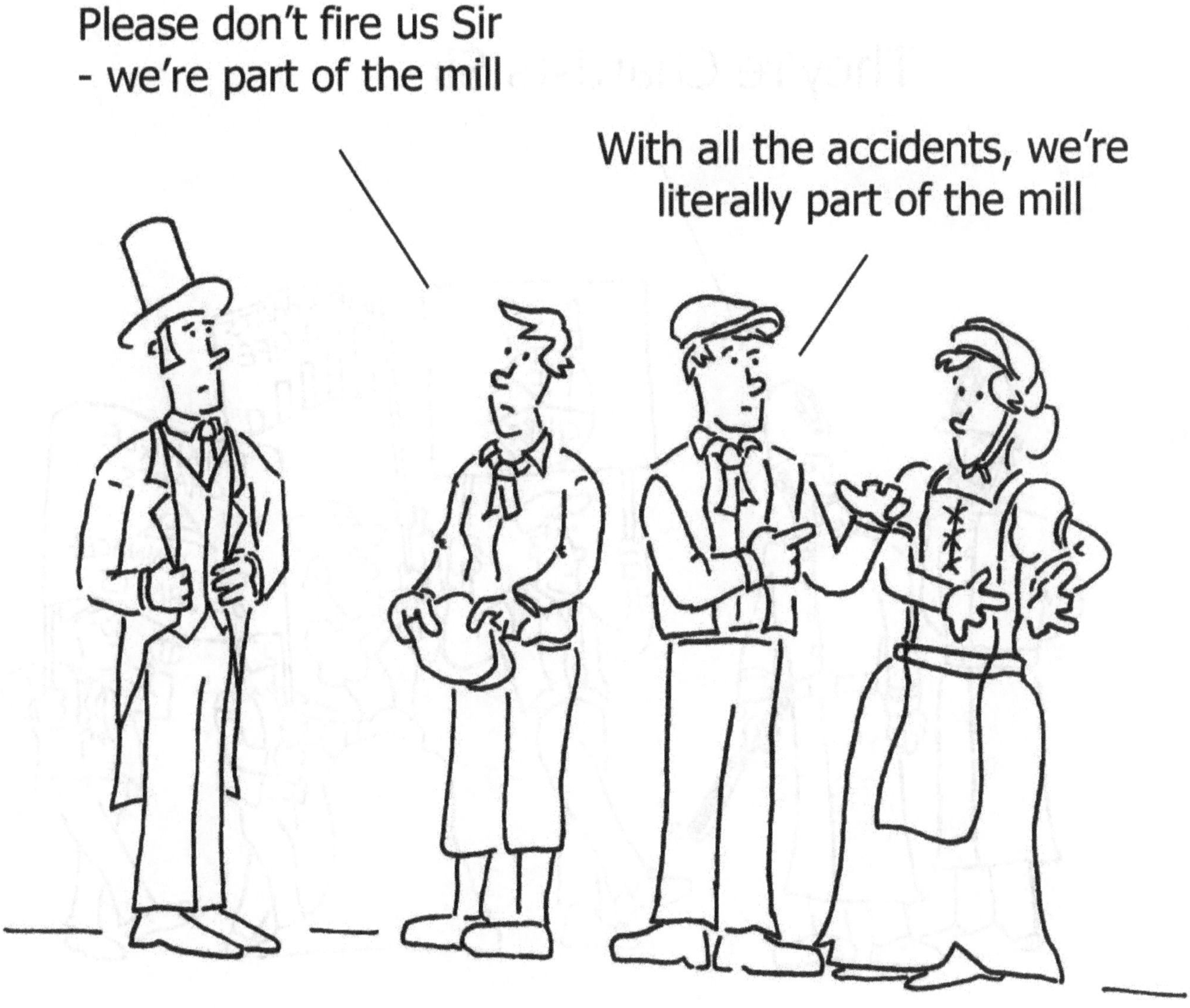
Please don't fire us Sir - we're part of the mill
With all the accidents, we're literally part of the mill

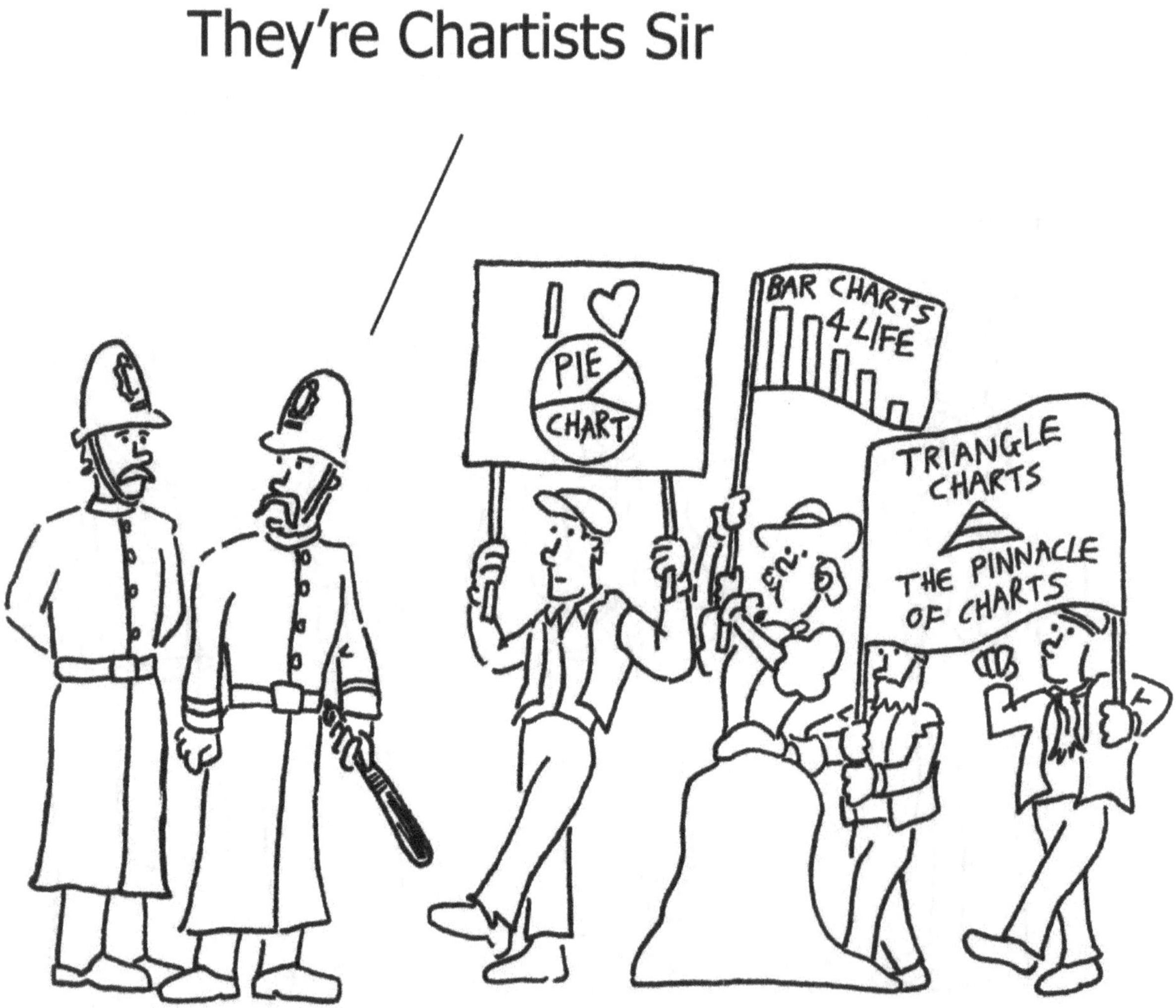
They're Chartists Sir
I ♥ PIE CHART
BAR CHARTS 4 LIFE
TRIANGLE CHARTS
THE PINNACLE OF CHARTS

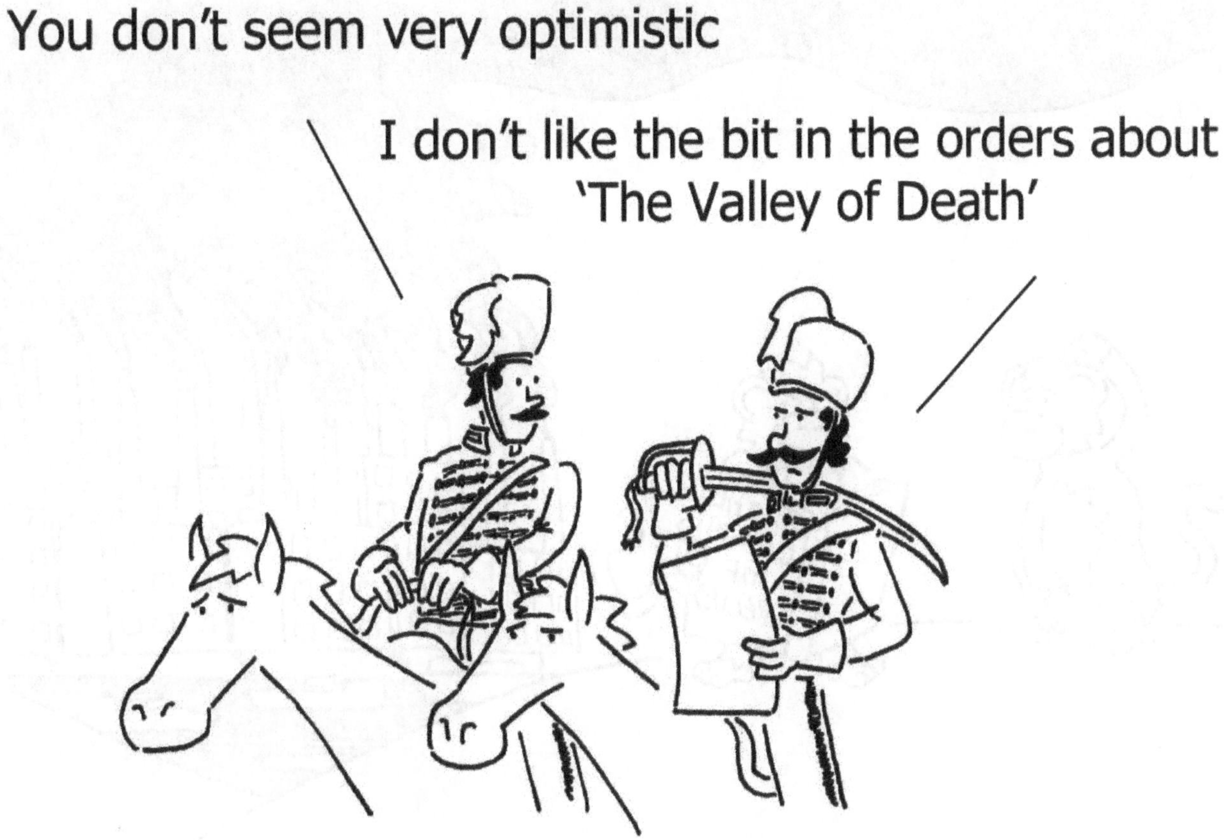
You don't seem very optimistic
I don't like the bit in the orders about 'The Valley of Death'

Balaclava 1854

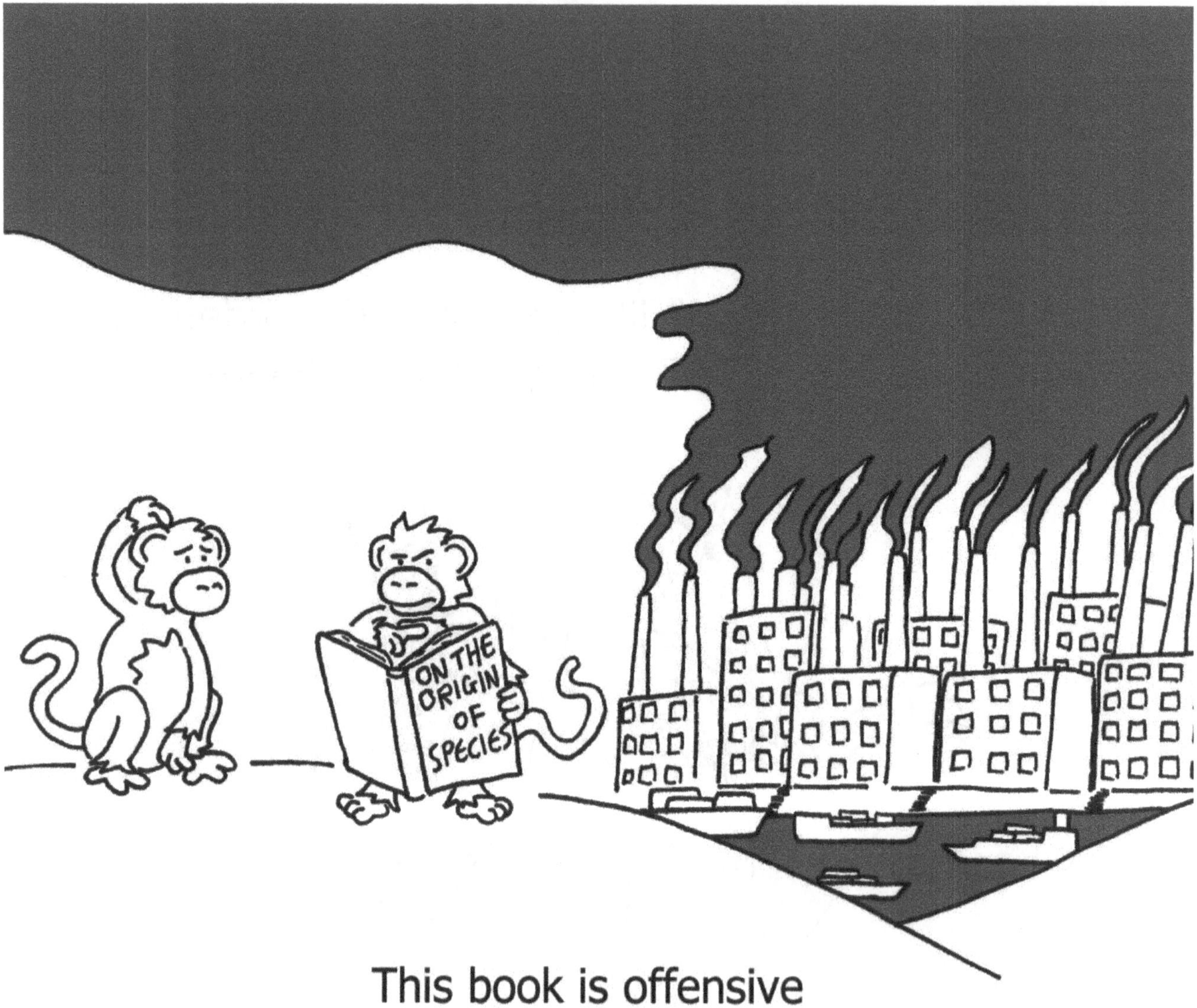
ON THE ORIGIN OF SPECIES

This book is offensive
- to suggest we're related to that species!

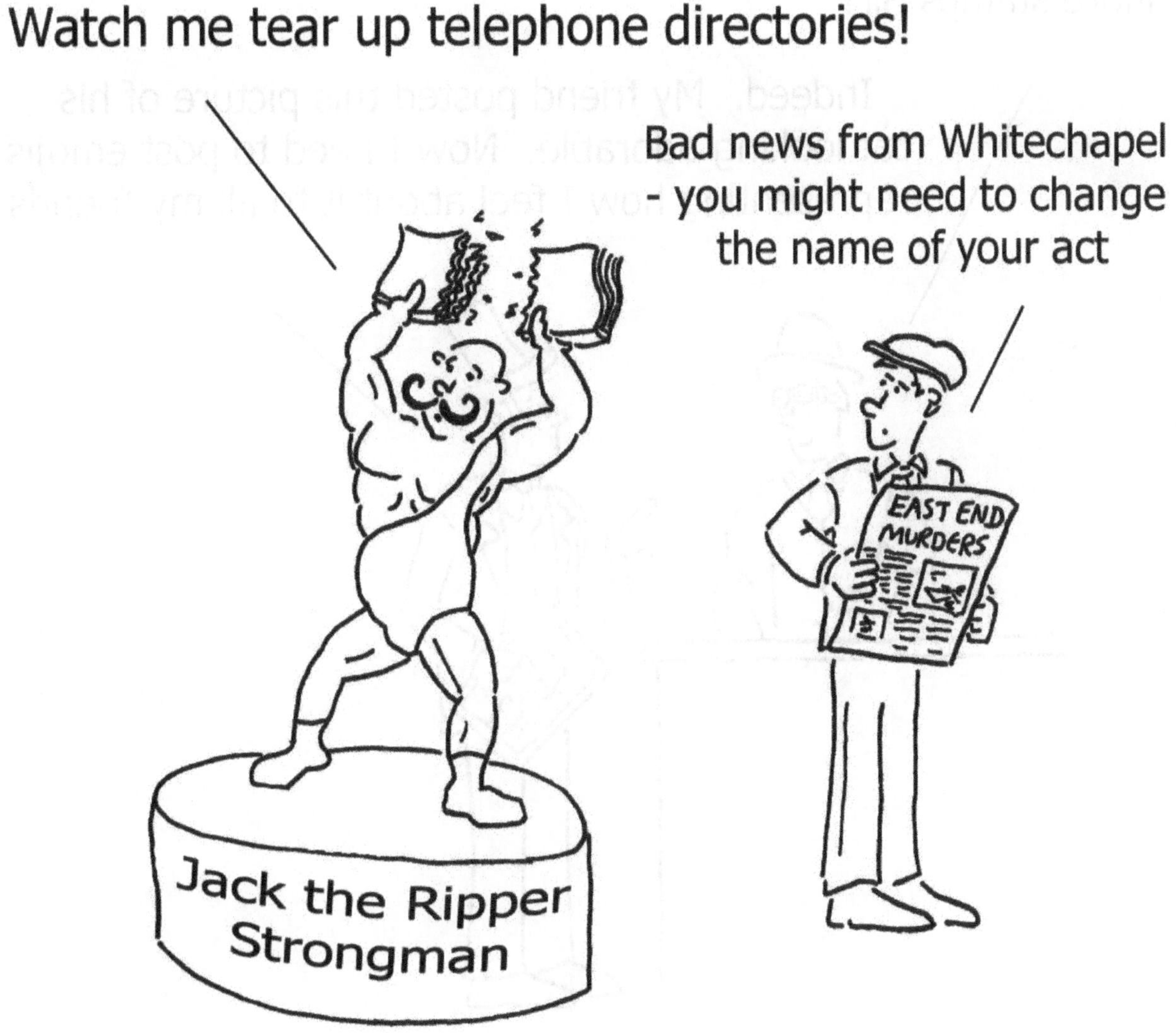
Watch me tear up telephone directories!
Bad news from Whitechapel - you might need to change the name of your act
Jack the Ripper Strongman
EAST END MURDERS

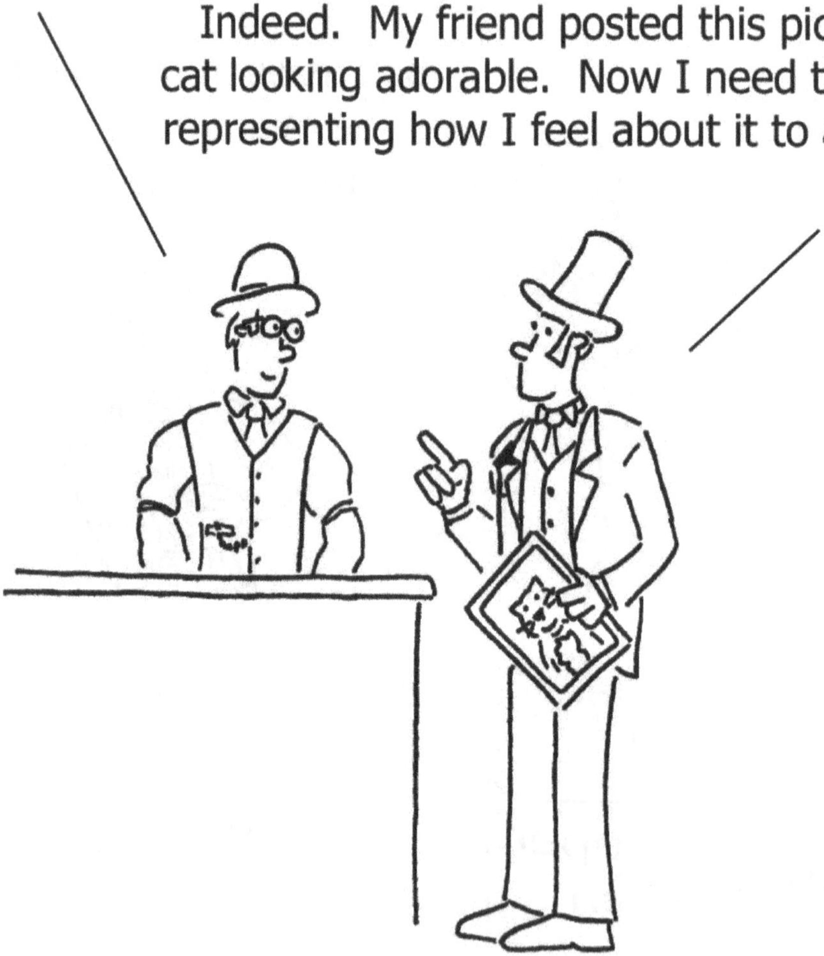
More stamps Sir?
Indeed. My friend posted this picture of his cat looking adorable. Now I need to post emojis representing how I feel about it to all my friends

Penny Post catches on

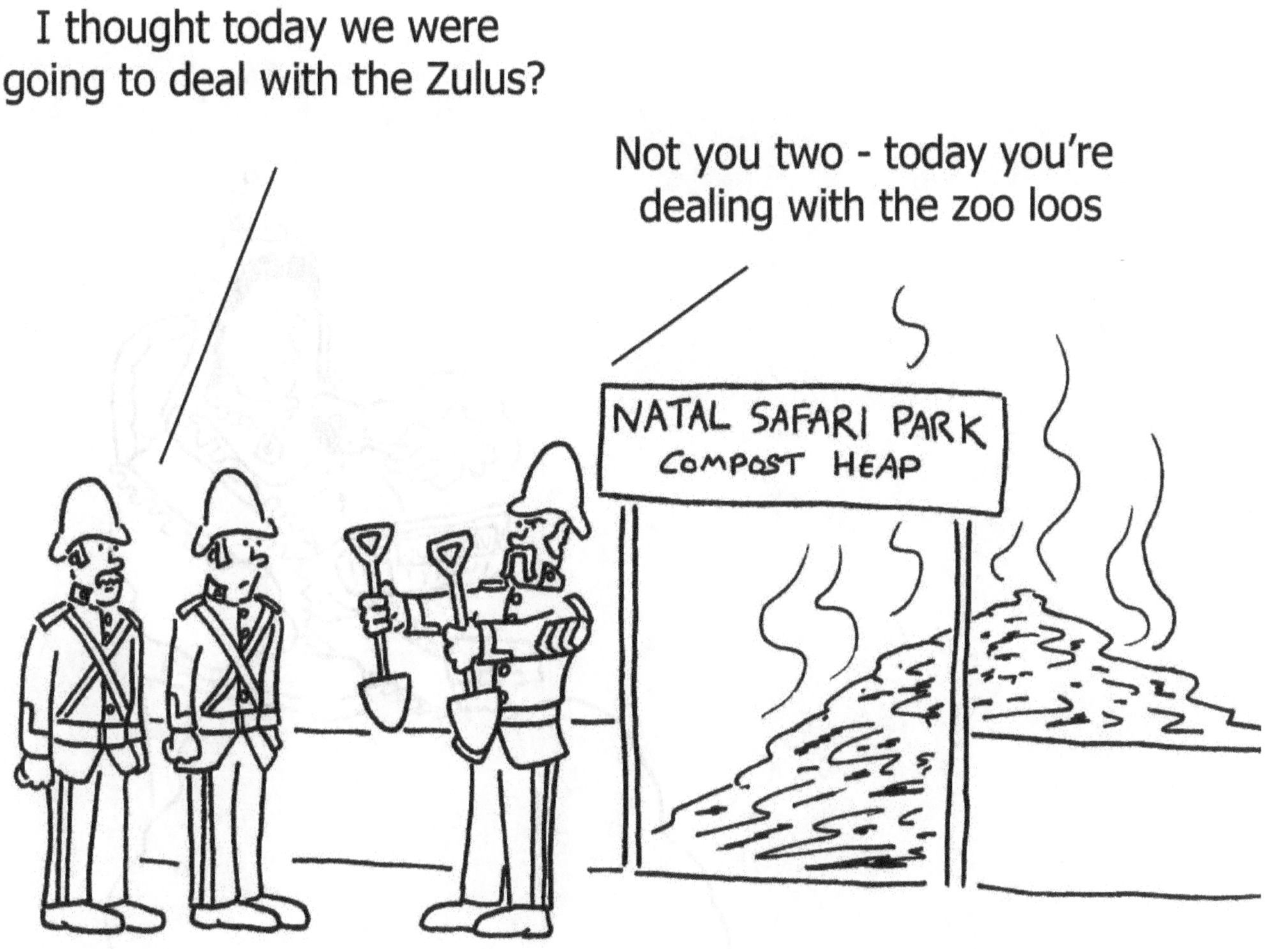
I thought today we were going to deal with the Zulus?
Not you two - today you're dealing with the zoo loos
NATAL SAFARI PARK
COMPOST HEAP

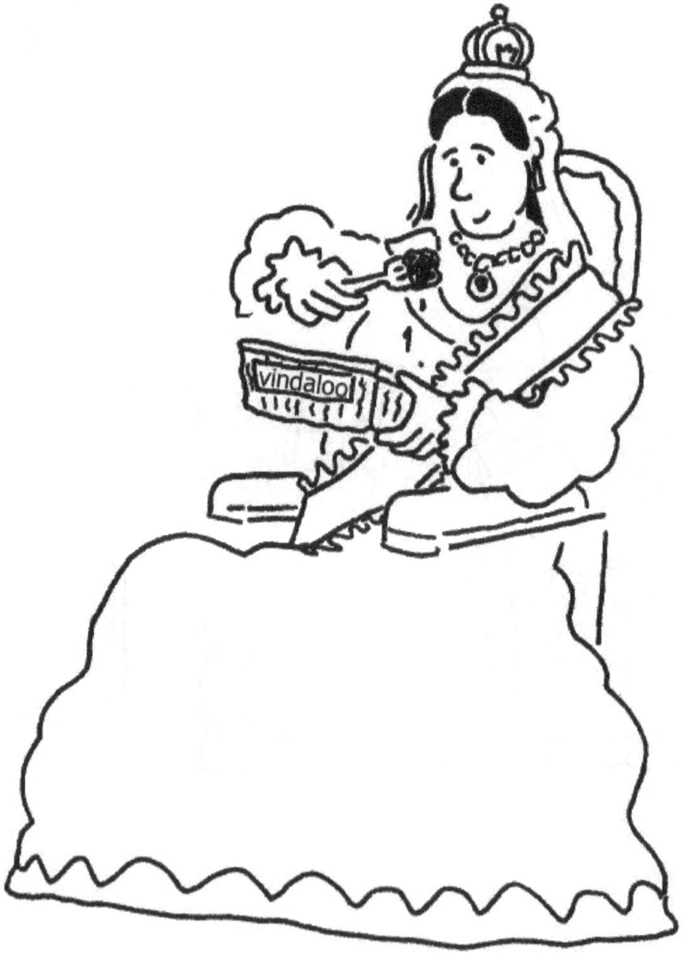
vindaloo

The Twentieth Century

The twentieth century appears rather full. The literacy of the population, the technology available to record sights and sounds, and the desire to document history was unprecedented.

There are eyewitness accounts of the 'Dambusters' raid, recorded crew interviews, photographs of the targets, written orders and reports, and over 130 relevant books. Compare the amount of information available on this raid to that which exists concerning the Viking raid on Lindisfarne.

That said, this full century is somewhat dominated by two major events (Dambusters might be a clue to one of them). Though to many a single encounter between England and (West) Germany in 1966 may define the century, it is the two World Wars waged by Britain against Germany and her allies which stand out.

Though terrible, these two wars moulded British character considerably. Most notably the stoic, stand-alone mentality demonstrated during the Battle of Britain and the black humour which helped to keep 'tommies' morale up and sanity intact whilst in the trenches.

Scientists will tell you we're made from stars. We are also made from history. I've had a bit of fun with the population of the past but they made us who we are and we should be grateful.

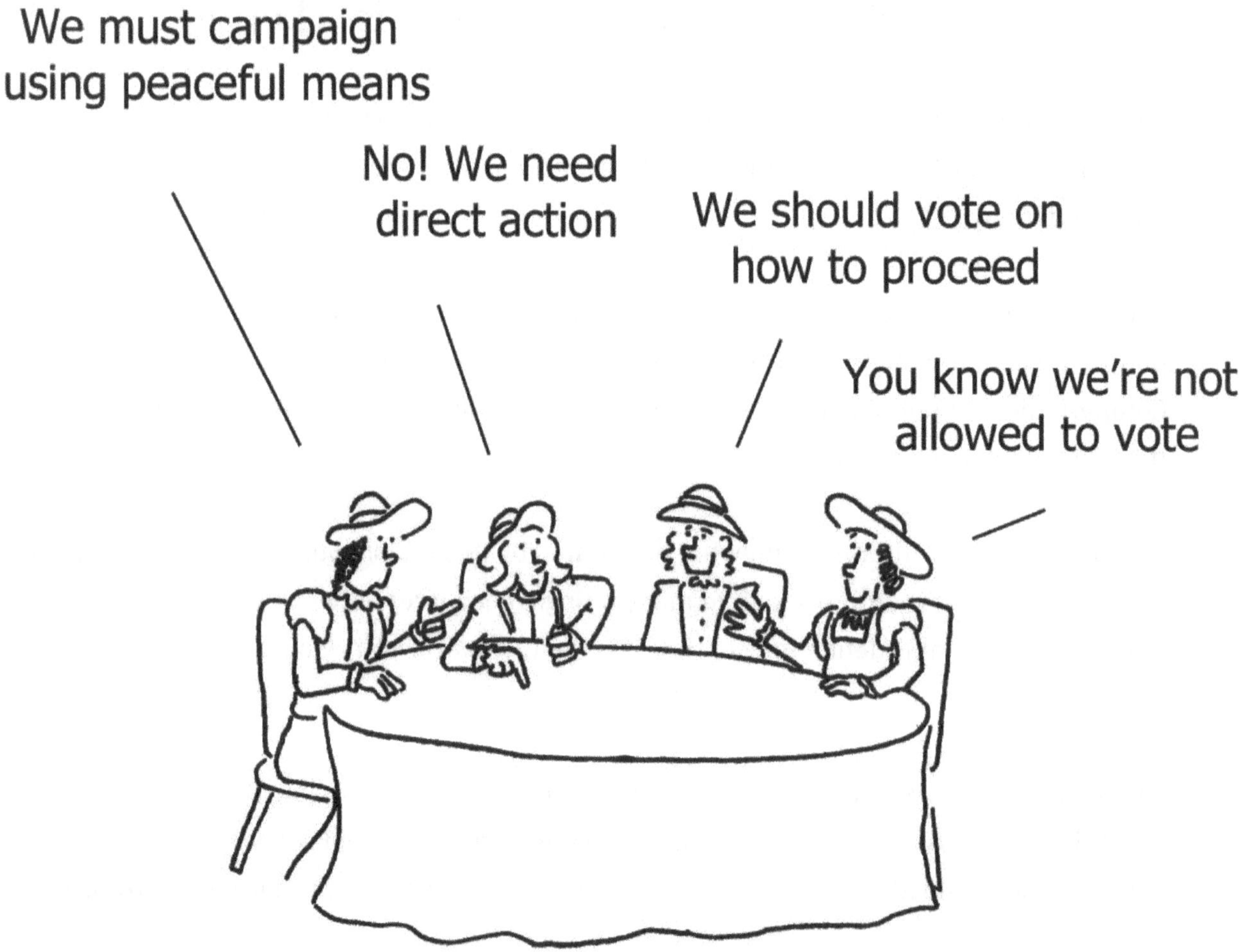
We must campaign using peaceful means
No! We need direct action
We should vote on how to proceed
You know we're not allowed to vote

Suffragettes/Suffragists

We’re out of ice for the champagne buckets.
Sail us close to one of those big ones and I’ll fill them up

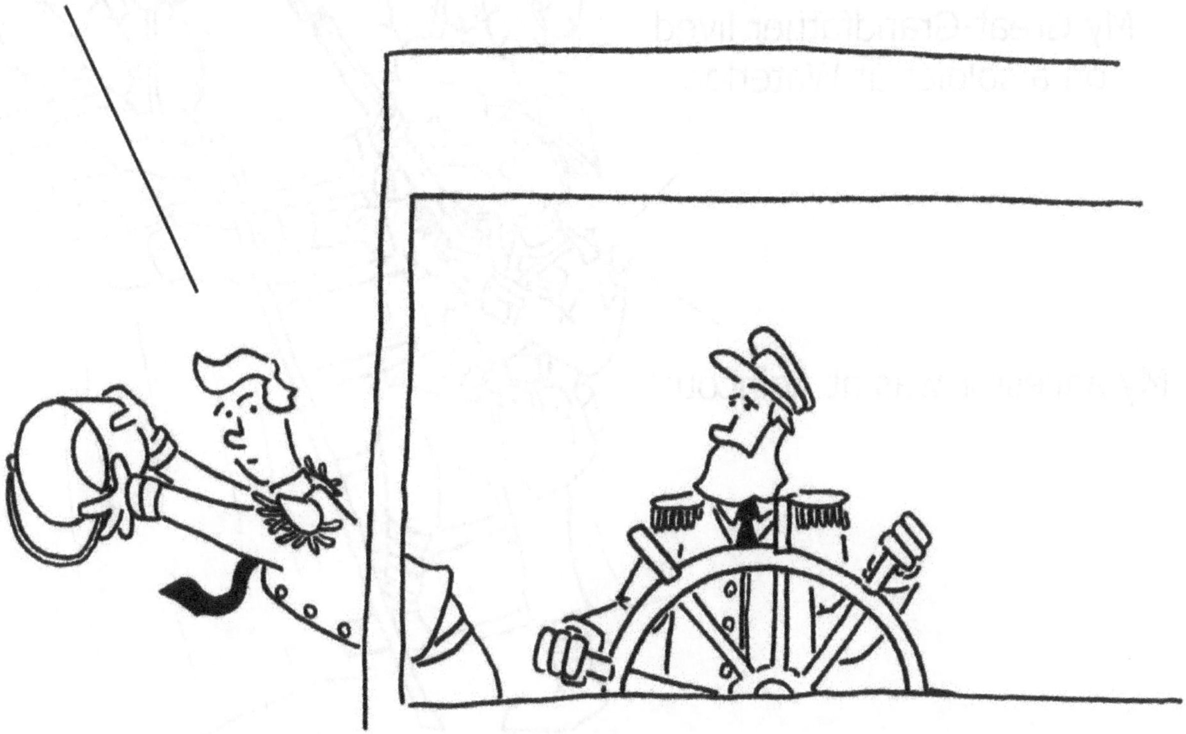

The Bridge of the Titanic

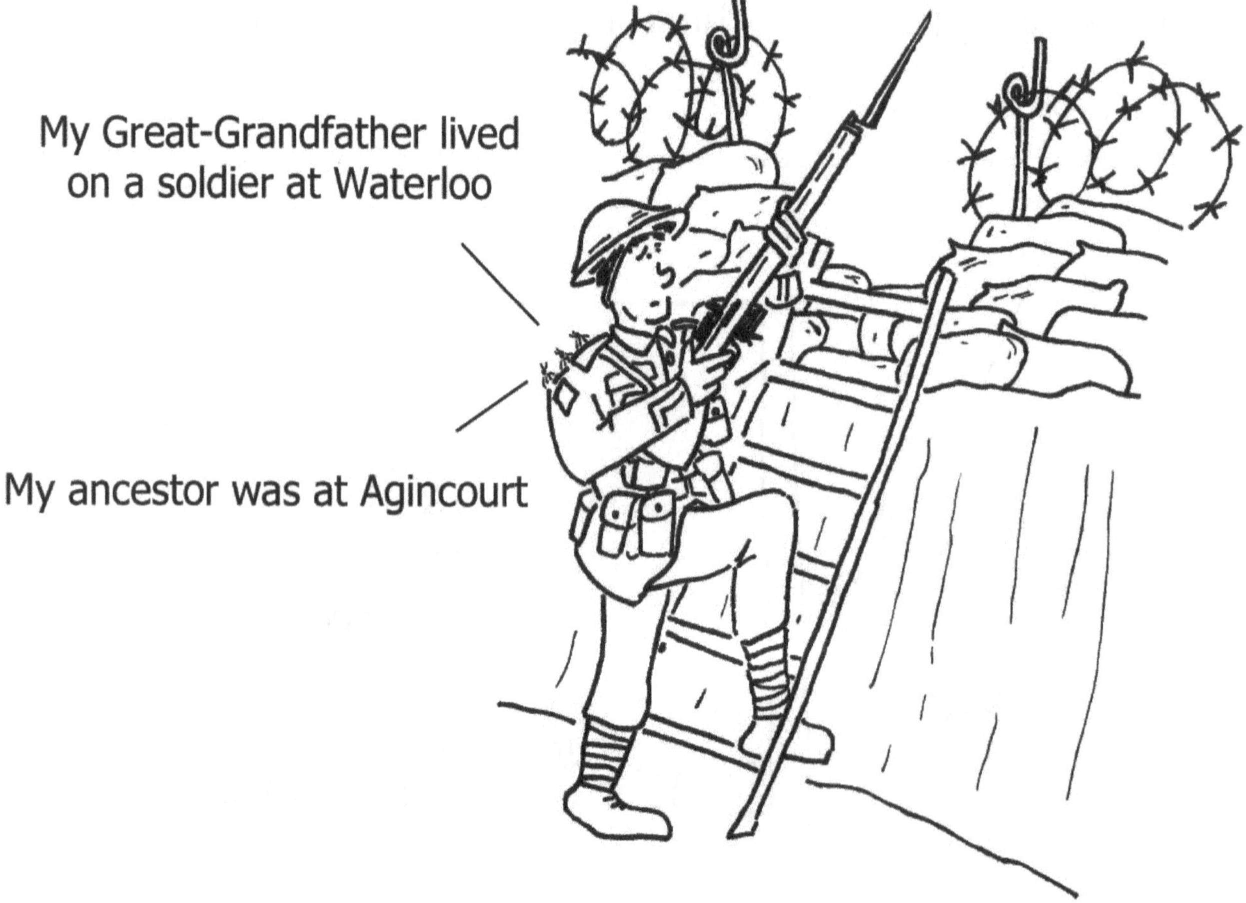
My Great-Grandfather lived
on a soldier at Waterloo
My ancestor was at Agincourt

Lice: one of history's constants

Sorry sir, that's the wrong piece of paper.
It's this one - the one about Coventry, Bristol
and the East End of London flattened in our time

I'm making the best of a bad situation

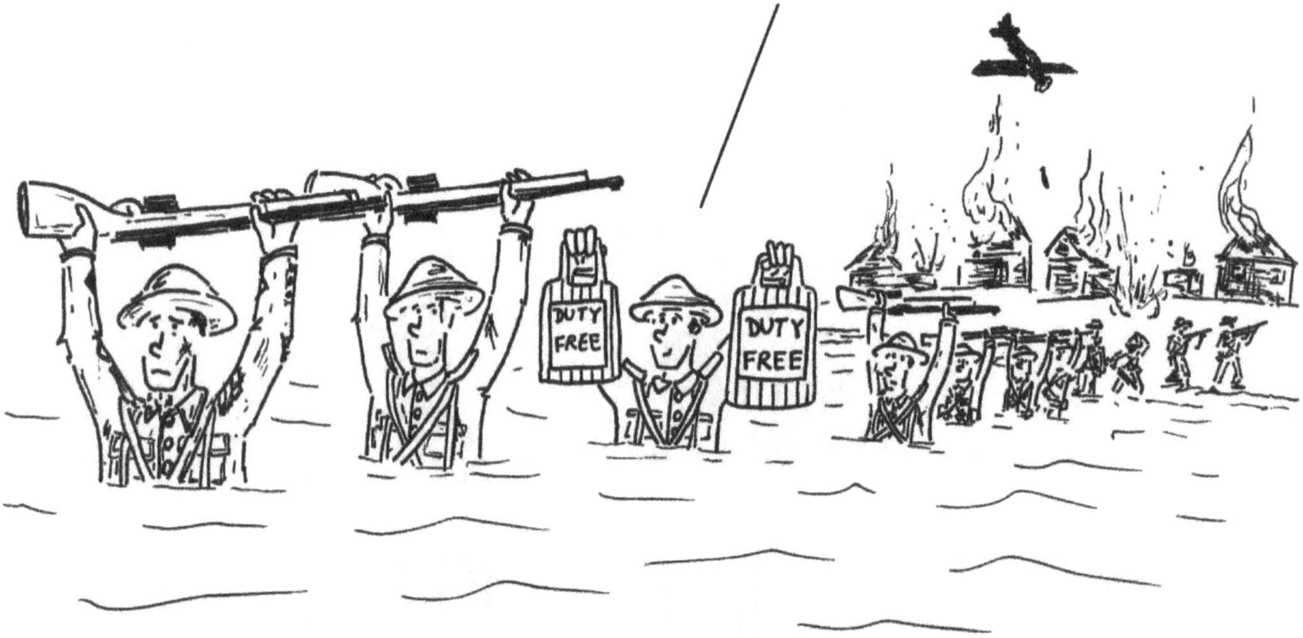
DUTY FREE
DUTY FREE

Dunkirk 1940

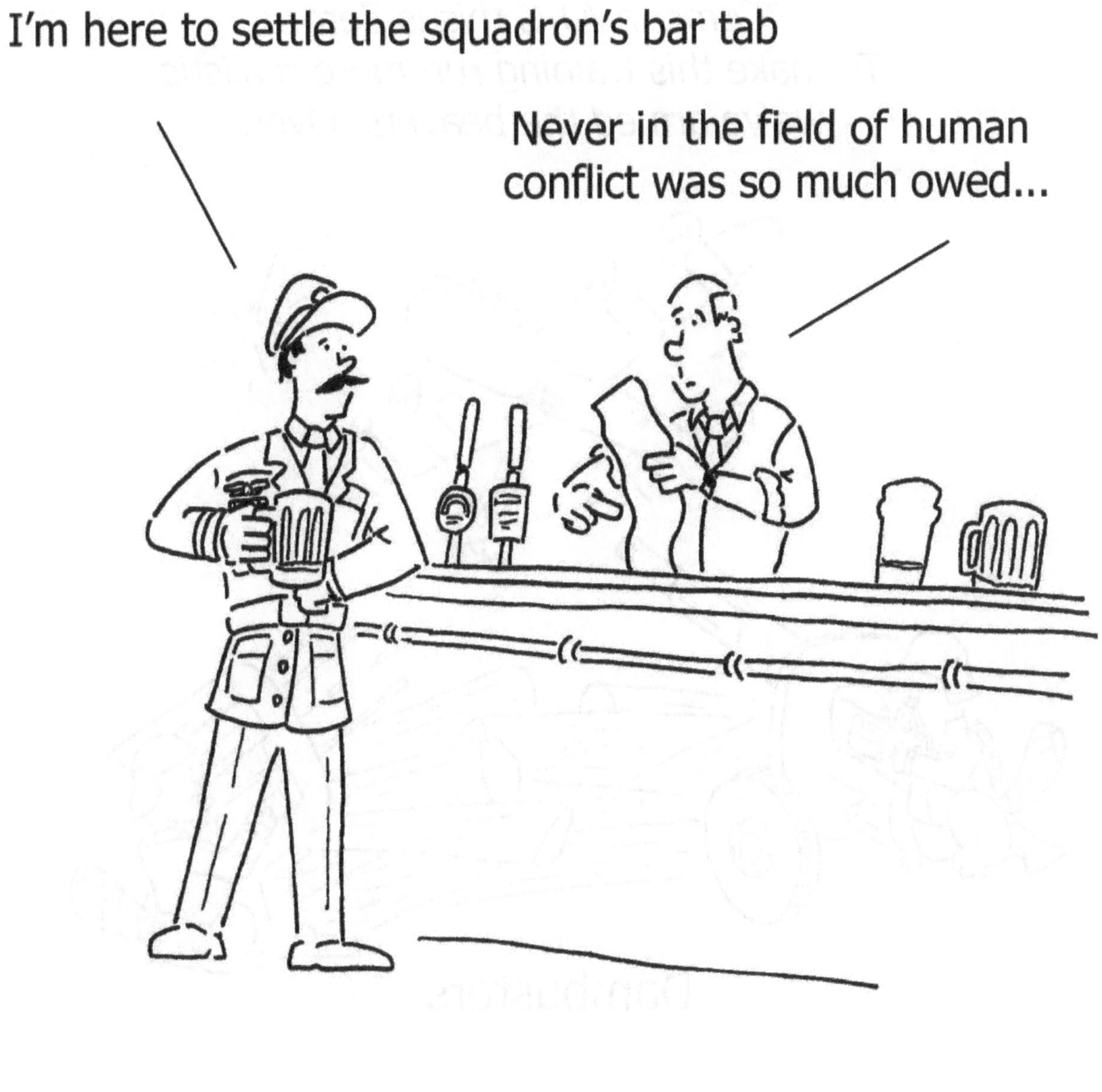
I'm here to settle the squadron's bar tab
Never in the field of human conflict was so much owed...

"Come in AJ-G this is Zero...
To make this training run more realistic
we've armed the beavers. Over."

Dambusters

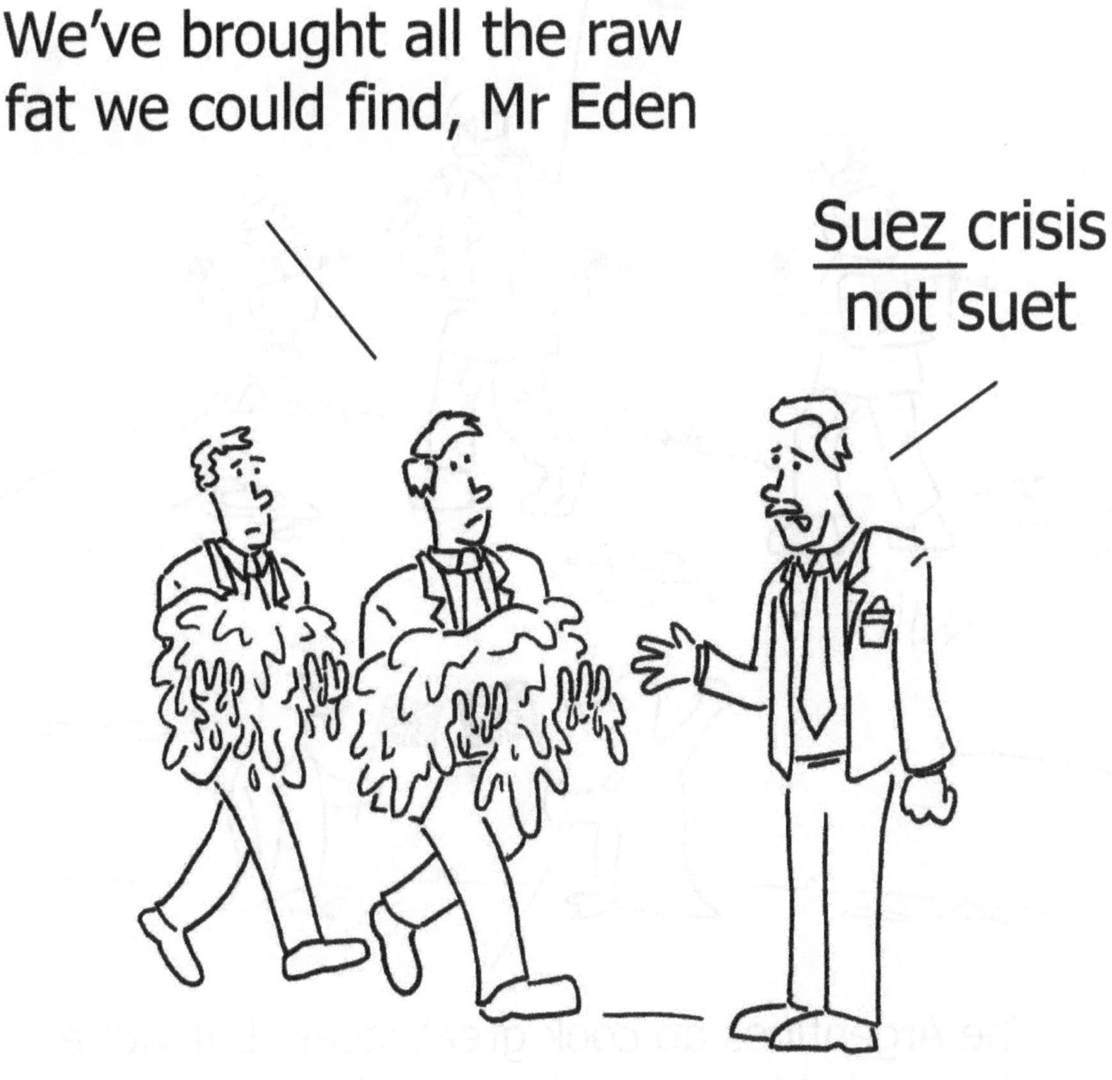
We've brought all the raw fat we could find, Mr Eden
Suez crisis not suet

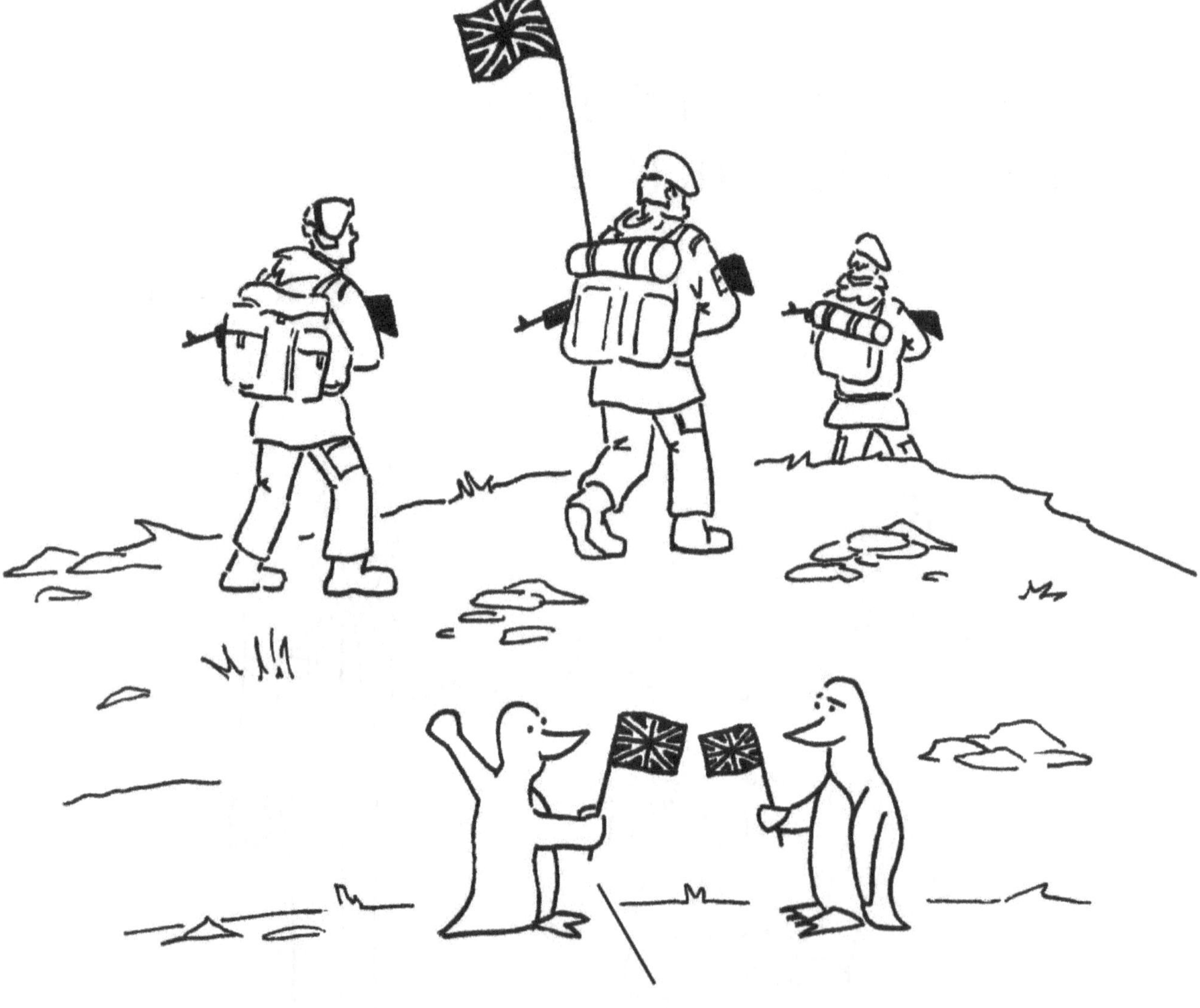

The Argentines do cook great steak, but we're fish and chip guys at heart really, aren't we?

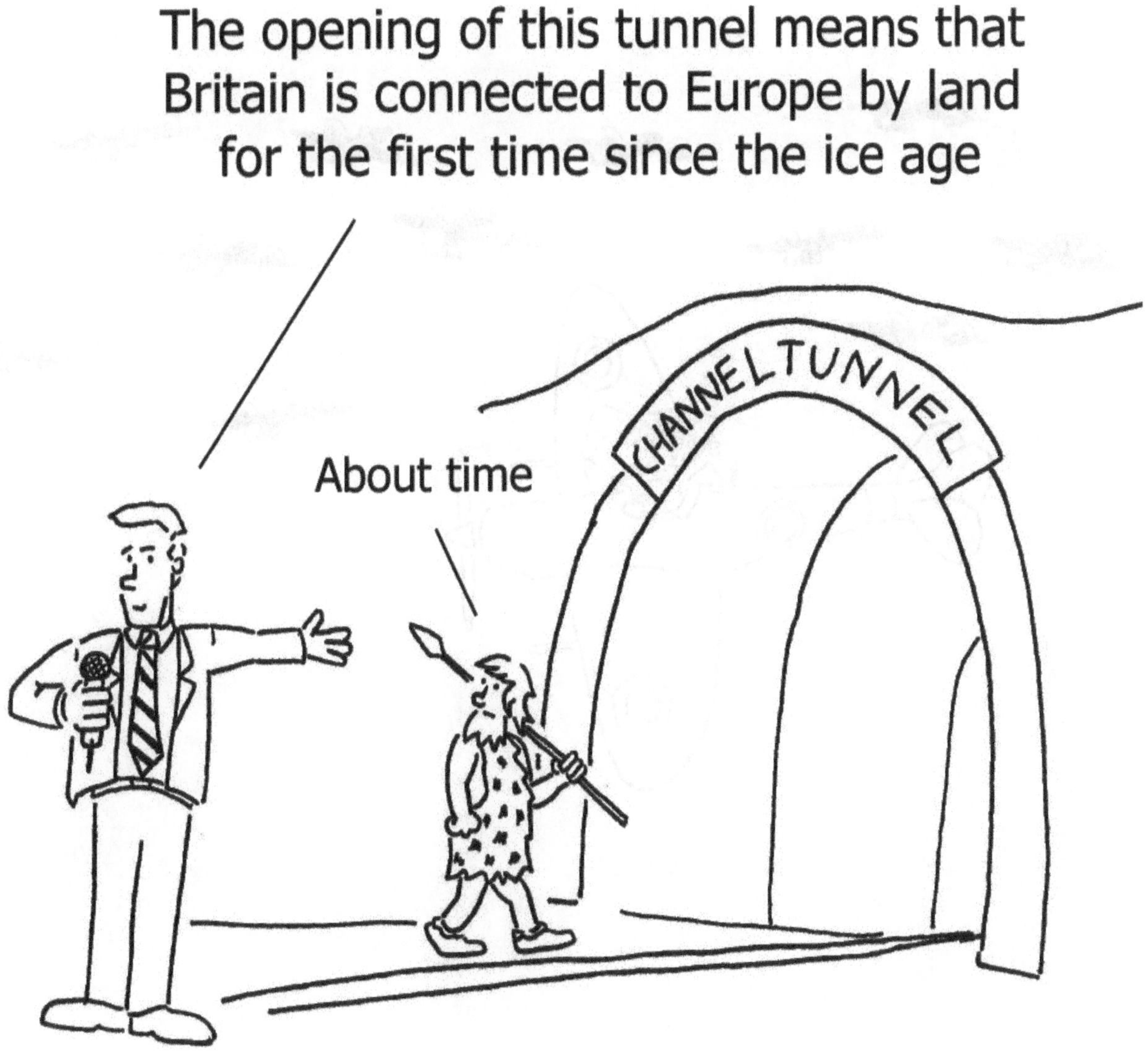
The opening of this tunnel means that Britain is connected to Europe by land for the first time since the ice age
About time
CHANNEL TUNNEL

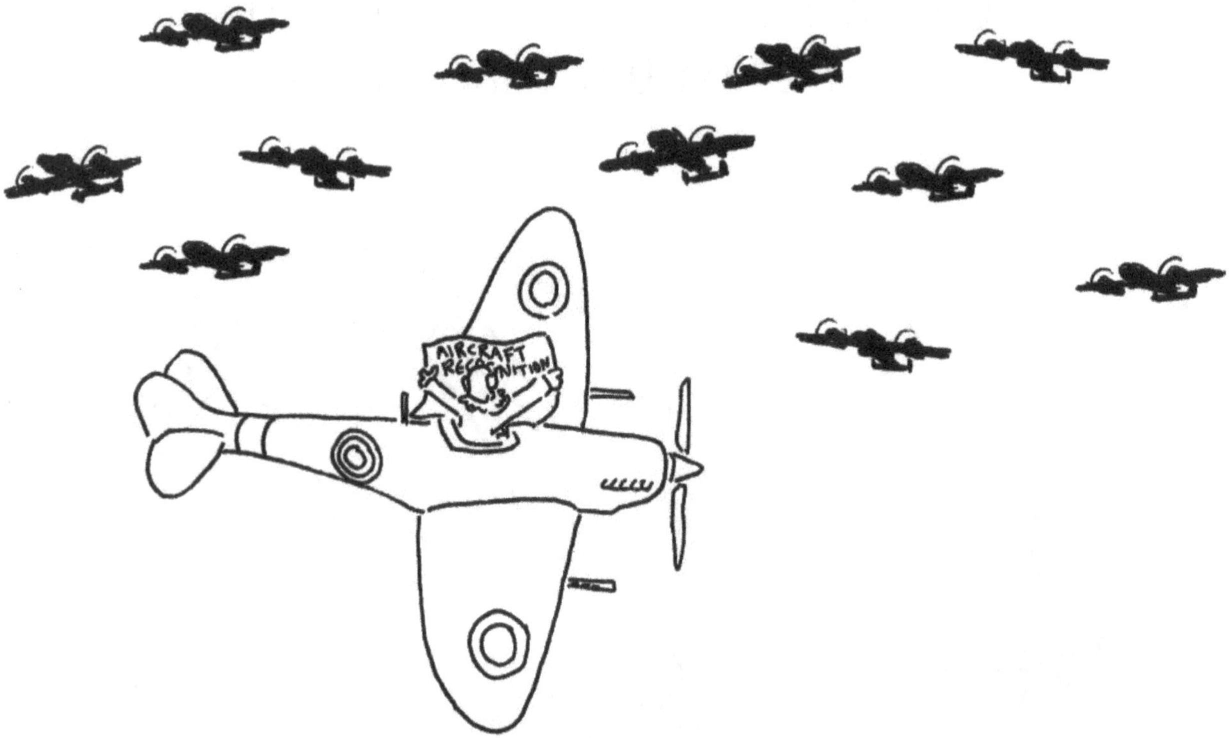
AIRCRAFT RECOGNITION

I hope you enjoyed the book!
Find out more about my books and services on
www.jamesmellorcreative.com
twitter: @jamesdfmellor
facebook: www.facebook.com/jamesmellorcreative

Thank you!